STARS AND STONES

An Astro-Magical Lapidary

Dedication
'To Anna'

Acknowledgements

I would like to thank Sue Ward for her professional editing work on the manuscript. Her insightful comments and suggestions led to many fruitful discussions, which, in turn, helped to improve the quality of this book.

STARS AND STONES

An Astro-Magical Lapidary

Peter Stockinger

Table of Contents

FOREWORD

Today few people attempt to defend astrology on scientific grounds, though in the past some were brave - or rash - enough to try. None was successful. And if astrology lacks any scientific basis, what hope is there for a book called "Stars and Stones"? For sceptics it beggars belief that a connection might prevail between the disposition of the planets and specific gemstones, let alone that this connection might extend also to us, influencing our life and our character.

As far back as the 6th Century BC, the Greek philosopher Thales, dubbed the Father of Science, argued that every event must have a natural, identifiable cause. And for him and his modern successors the influence of the stars on mundane events, being bereft of such a cause, must be non-existent. The possibility may well seem intriguing, at least in theory, but in practice it has no scientific backing at all.

No, Science, we're loftily assured, deals with the real world, basing itself on empirical evidence garnered through systematic observation, experimentation and careful measurement. To be accepted as valid, each and every hypothesis must be confirmed by rigorous testing, the results capable of being reproduced by anyone who follows the relevant procedures. These criteria are what astrology, according to its critics, has signally failed to meet. Even the statistical data once marshalled in its defence, notably the work of Michel Gauquelin in the nineteen-fifties, has been called into question. Astrology, it would seem, has no basis in reality.

Well, no basis in empirical reality, that much we have surely to concede. No basis, that is, in the reality our senses bring to our attention each day. Only when we examine that reality more carefully, when, that is, we look beyond what's immediately apparent, do we find that astrology may not be quite so daft - I mean "unscientific" - as its opponents maintain. Let me try to explain why.

Until recently scientists, taking their cue from Sir Isaac Newton, stoutly maintained that the things that constitute reality are material, separable from one another and quite independent of us. From this it follows that in so far as they affect one another, they do so by physical means and nothing else. Which, as we noted earlier, explains why the planets and their changing disposition in the sky have no bearing on our lives. Or, come to that, on gemstones or anything else. To that extent its critics are right.

The snag is that none of this is true. Thanks to particle physics we now know that reality's not a bit like what was just described. Missing from it, for a start, is any notion of "separability", the belief that an object can influence another only if there's some kind of physical contact, however tenuous or indirect, between the two. Instead, it has been demonstrated that on the quantum level, the very heart of reality, there prevails an inter-connectedness - an entanglement almost - which classical physics, the sort that derives from Newton, never remotely suspected.

Not that defenders of the old-fashioned view have given up without a fight. Until recently they sought to argue that what might be true on the microscopic level was not relevant to anything beyond it. Their suggestion was that the quirks and anomalies recorded there manage somehow to right themselves before graduating to the "real" world that we inhabit. This argument never made sense and, perhaps not surprisingly, is encountered less often today. After all there's no sound reason to believe that what's true at the microscopic level isn't true elsewhere, even if its behaviour remains as yet undetected. On top of which quantum experiments have by now moved from the microscopic environment to one more similar to, if not yet the same as, the macroscopic one inhabited by us. It is no longer unreasonable to suggest that all things are interconnected. Neither is it unreasonable to suggest that astrology derives from, as well as exploits, this universal connectedness.

Working in its favour also is a second discovery concerning the nature of reality, one that demolishes the mechanistic view that the physical world, self-contained and self-sufficient, is the only one that exists, with, it follows, nothing more beyond it. What quantum physics has disclosed is that reality not only contains but also transcends the physical world, with events in both determined to some extent by us. In other words we unconsciously participate in the workings of a universe whose parts, as we noted earlier, are all interconnected.

All of which reflects and to some extent confirms the view of those who, even in Ancient Greece, challenged the mechanistic approach recommended by people like Thales, one defended since then by all who remain committed to the "scientific" method . Not that their approach was unwelcome. On the contrary we have all benefited from the discoveries it enabled scientists to make, notably after it got the upper hand in the seventeenth century, putting paid to the errors and superstitions that prevailed until then. Astrology, more's the pity, was one of the casualties also. A pity because we know now that its basic premise is fully consistent with what reality has since revealed itself to be. By contrast classical science, however well it works in practice, got things badly wrong.

For astrologers, as the author explains in this intriguing book, reality is both One and Many. Or, rather, it is viewed as the One expressing itself through the Many that comprise it. That most of us overlook this implicit oneness, while aware of its myriad components, is because our perception is limited to what our senses equip us to discover. Denied to us - well, to most of us at least - is direct access to the absolute reality proposed by quantum physics, one whose abstract symmetries dwell outside space and time but are somehow influenced by us and, it goes without saying, influence each of us in turn. It is in this underlying "oneness" and, implicitly, the interconnectedness of its parts that astrology finds its justification.

It is this interconnectedness that explains the affinities astrologers identify between individual planets and mundane objects such as gemstones. At first glimpse this may seem pretty arbitrary, even superstitious, but it is nothing of the sort. Yes, it may well be that hundreds, nay thousands, of years ago, someone first listed these correspondences, but he or she may have had sound reasons for doing so. The fundamental unity of existence - where all is in each and each in all - does at least endow them with a theoretical validity. Happily experience down the centuries has demonstrated their practical validity as well.

Best of all, the information given in this book will enable readers to test that validity for themselves. I am confident they will not be disappointed.

David Conway
Machynlleth

July 2014

INTRODUCTION

For the unity of the form, the duality of the matter, the trinity of the composition and the quaternity of the composite when they are added make a total of ten. (Robert Grosseteste)

My main inspiration for writing this book was to reintroduce the reader to the idea of correspondences and correlations between planets and gemstones. Although they are now largely forgotten, these correspondences were commonly known and used throughout centuries past; the chapter about planets and gemstones will discuss these in detail. This book will also show how we can all benefit in our everyday lives from this long lost knowledge. Although lapidaries have a long history and can be traced as far back as at least the third century BC, they generally began to fall out of favour during the 17th century. At the same time, traditional Western astrology, informed by Hermetic and Neo-Platonist theories, was being marginalised by the ever-growing influence of scientific rationalism. This influence can be epitomised by the foundation of the Royal Society in 1662. Although undergoing a partial renaissance in the 19th century, astrology never recovered to its former popularity/glory/position. Some would explain this by the fact that it had lost its status as an integral part of the magical arts. Throughout this book, many techniques used in traditional Western astrology, as it was practised until the end of the 17th century, are reintroduced. To gain a better understanding of why the basic concept of astrology is of such great importance, we have to look far back in time and begin with the question of the creation of the universe.

The Creation of the Universe

Aristotle brought the question of the creation of the universe to the point when he wrote in his *Metaphysics:*

> "Then comes the most difficult of all questions, whether unity or being, as the Pythagoreans and Plato said, is not a particular something at all, but is the very being of any being."

The multi-talented Renaissance astrologer, geographer, mathematician and imperialist Dr. John Dee, who, having studied the teachings of Aristotle at Trinity College, Cambridge, became a Platonist in later life, wrote in the 8th theorem of his *Monas Hieroglyphica:*

"Besides, a cabbalistic expansion of the quarternary, in accordance with the customary style of numeration (when we say, one, two, three, four), produces, in sum, the denary, as Pythagoras himself used to say; for 1, 2, 3, and 4, add up to ten."

With this theorem Dee demonstrates his familiarity with the teachings of the Pythagoreans as well as Plato's cosmology as expressed in the *Timaeus*. The understanding of the cabbalistic extension of the quarternary is the key to understanding the creation of the universe, the four elements and the working principles of astrology itself. All this knowledge lies hidden in the symbol of the decad, also known as the Pythagorean Tetractys.

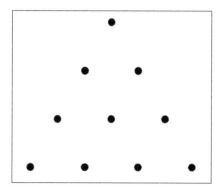

The point of absolute Unity is represented by the • at the apex of the Tetractys. It is eternal, stable and incomprehensible. It may be called God of Gods. Whenever it contemplates itself, it splits into two and creates the world. This primordial scission is represented by the second row of the Tetractys. What can clearly be seen here is the fact that, first of all, creation is division. The One does not procreate; it is. But to procreate, there have to be three principles in one, called the ternary or creative foundation. In other words, after the primordial scission or division follows the addition, the joining of what had separated with the original cause.

In the *Timaeus* of Plato, Timaeus explains the creation of the cosmos as the manifestation, or outward projection, of the One through polarity, as follows:

14

"Now that which comes to be must be bodily, and so visible and tangible; and nothing can be visible without fire, or tangible without something solid, and nothing is solid without earth. Hence the god, when he began to put together the body of the universe, set about making it of fire and earth."

But, as we have already seen, the polarity of fire and earth:

"... cannot be satisfactorily united without a third; for there must be some bond between them drawing them together."

And therefore, the "maker":

" ... set water and air between fire and earth, and made them so far as was possible, proportional to one another, so that as fire is to air, so is air to water, and as air is to water, so is water to earth, and thus he bound together the frame of a world visible and tangible."

In this way the quarternary comes into being and is represented by the bottom row of the Tetractys. Timeaeus continues, saying that:

"... for these reasons, and from such constituents, four in number, the body of the universe was brought into being, coming into concord by means of proportion, and from this it acquired Love."

Having now explained the meaning of the numbers 1, 2, 3, and 4, we can add the numbers of this progressive triangle resulting in the number ten; it is this triangle 'ten' that contains all the possibilities of the universe.

To sum up: we can now state that the forms engendered by the Tetractys are:

The triangle: the first possible surface which is the result of an addition.

The square: resulting from the first possible number to be multiplied, number two. All material existence is based upon the square.

The circle: absolute Unity which is in itself eternal, therefore all life is cyclical.

All other existing forms are born out of the triangle, square or circle.

The Four Elements

In *The Theology of Arithmetic*, attributed to the Neo-Platonist Iamblichus of Chalcis we read:

"And there are evidently also four elements and their powers, which are disposed in things according to the nature of the tetrad."

As it is all encompassing, the Tetractys, or decade, contains the four elements, the basic building blocks of the manifest world.

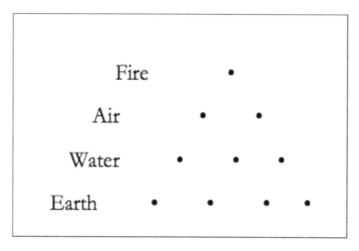

Fire, the first element, the One, is the cause of all. When it manifests, it becomes three, or the element of Water, the inversion of Fire, its opposite. Twice Fire equals Air and twice Air equals the element of Earth.

These are the symbols of the four elements:

To distinguish and recognise the four elements, one must look at their inherent qualities. There are four basic qualities matter can have, namely: hot, cold, moist and dry.

 Fire is hot and dry

 Air is hot and moist

 Water is cold and moist, the opposite of Fire

 Earth is cold and dry, the opposite of Air

The Pentactys

Having examined the four elements, we can now go forward one step and extend the mystical Tetractys into the Pentactys which reveals that the divine creative triangle is surrounded by the twelve manifestations of the world.

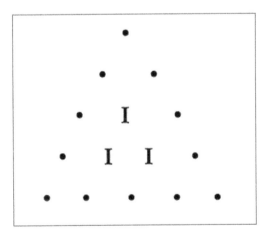

The Pentactys can be depicted in a more familiar way as the wheel of the Zodiac:

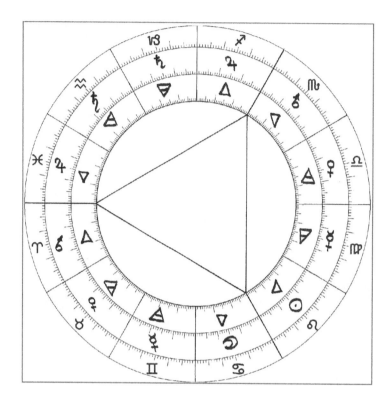

The circle is divided through the diameter into two, representing the opposites of male and female, dark and light and so on, and then into four through the elements, whereby the three principles preside over each element, bringing the total number to twelve.

We can see that the twelve signs of the zodiac can be divided into four groups of three signs, thus:

△	♈	♌	♐
△	♎	♒	Ⅱ
▽	♋	♏	♓
▽	♑	♉	♍

Aries, Libra, Cancer, and Capricorn are the moveable signs;

Leo, Aquarius, Scorpio and Taurus are the fixed signs;

Sagittarius, Gemini, Pisces and Virgo are the mutable or double-bodied signs;

There is one moveable, one fixed and one mutable sign in each element.

The Planets

Like the signs of the zodiac, the planets correspond to one element each:

Saturn ♄: is cold and dry and is therefore attributed to the element of earth;

Jupiter ♃: is hot and moist and is attributed to the element of air;

Venus ♀: is cold and moist and is attributed to the element of water;

Mars ♂: is hot and dry and is attributed to the element of fire;

Mercury ☿: is cold and dry and is attributed to the element of earth;

The Sun ☉: is hot and dry and is attributed to the element of fire;

The Moon ☽: is cold and moist and is attributed to the element of water.

ঌৄৎ

Case Study A - Ken

Ken, a man in his early forties at the time of the consultation, is a highly intelligent and an intensely spiritual person. Mercury and Venus are the strongest planets in his nativity which is shown below.

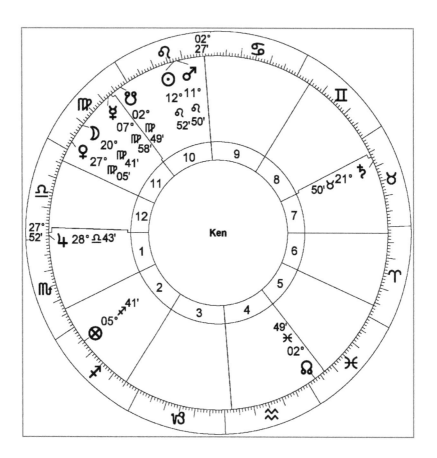

Ken stated his problem in the following way:

"My entire life I have felt a deficit of personal power, ambition, willpower and warrior energy. I am pretty cold and intellectual most of the time in my relationships."

Ken's temperament was calculated and is shown in the table below.

		S	C	M	P
Rising Sign	Libra	2			
Its Lord	Venus				1
Moon Sign	Virgo			2	
Its Lord	Mercury			1	
Moon Phase	1/4	1			
QAS	Summer		2		
Sun Sign	Leo		1		
Its Lord	Sun		1		
LoG	Mercury			1	
Score		3	4	4	2

Immediately apparent is that his temperament is a mix between the melancholic and the choleric, with some traces of the sanguine temperament included. We remember what we said about the choleric temperament before:

"The choleric temperament combines the primary qualities of hot and dry and is associated with the element of fire. People whose temperament is mainly choleric are enthusiastic, optimistic, assertive, often aggressive. They are always ready for action, enterprising and enthusiastic, often impatient."

This is in stark contrast to the temperament of the melancholic:

"The melancholic temperament consists of the primary qualities of cold and dry and is associated with the element of earth. Typical melancholics are analytical, studious people who can be very antisocial. Coming over as reserved, they can easily be underestimated or overlooked. Melancholics are generally very patient but their rigidity, due to the cold quality, can make them pessimistic, melancholic and even depressed."

Adding to this the hot and moist qualities of the sanguine temperament, we can see that the hot quality of the choleric and the sanguine has to be investigated closely. A look at the dignity and debility levels of Ken's planets helped to clarify the picture even further.

Planet	Sign	Score
☉	12♌52	11
☽	20♏41	4
☿	07♏58	26
♀	27♏05	16
♂	11♌50	3
♃	28♎43	15
♄	21♉50	7

All the planets in Ken's chart have positive values and even Venus, the only planet essentially debilitated by being in her fall, is saved by her location in the 11th house and other positive factors. What we can see though, is the fact that Mars is the weakest planet of the chart. He is also combust, being overshadowed and weakened by Ken's strong Sun. To remedy this, the Mars stones garnet, haematite, jasper, or magnetite were prescribed.

PART ONE –

THE ASTROLOGICAL BASICS

Divers Effects of the stars are drawn forth from the stars, according to the various dispositions of the matter; whereof the Astrologer ought very well to examine the several natures and qualities of the subjects receiving. (William Lilly)

Before proceeding further, I have to point out that the models given below describe the universe in astrological terms, differing entirely from the model currently used by the scientific community. The current scientific image of the solar system shows the Sun at the centre and the eight known planets orbiting around it. This is a representation of the objective reality of our solar system and, although this may be correct from a scientific point of view, it does not depict the universe as observed by the astrologer. The main difference is that in astrology the basic observational point is the Earth. Put into other words, we could say that in the astrological model the planets appear to move around the Earth and are therefore described as if observed by a terrestrial viewer. This is called the geocentric perspective and is diametrically opposed to the heliocentric perspective, currently embraced by the scientific community. It is very important to understand that both of these systems represent the same reality and that it is only the point of view that divides them. The heliocentric model describes the universe as it would be seen from an outsider's point of view, a remote onlooker, positioned far away from our solar system. The geocentric model, on the other hand, displays the same universe, but shows the sky and the planets just as they can be observed by anybody observing from Earth. A perfect depiction of the astrological universe can be found in what are known as the celestial spheres or the celestial orbs.

Peter Apian: *Cosmographia*, Antwerp, 1539

From the diagram above of the celestial spheres, it is obvious that the Earth is in the centre of the spheres and therefore at the centre of the universe. The Earth is separated into four layers, corresponding to the four elements. Around it, grouped into concentric circles, are the nine spheres or orbs. These comprise the seven spheres of the planets, Luna, Mercury, Venus, Sun, Mars, Jupiter and Saturn. Thereafter we find the sphere of the fixed stars and the sphere of the constellations. The outermost sphere is called *Primum Mobile*, creating the primary motion that causes the rotation of the heavens. This primary motion is of the utmost importance because it carries the planets, stars, Sun and Moon around the Earth marking the passage of the day. From a practical point of view it is this motion that is responsible for the planets' rising, culminating and setting which, consequently, determines their accidental strengths and weaknesses, or, in other words, their ability to act.

The Elements

As mentioned above, the terrestrial world consists of four elements, called earth, air, water and fire. These can be seen as the primary forces on Earth upon which the planets act. The elements are composed of the four fundamental principles, also known as *primary*

24

qualities. These are called hot, cold, moist and dry. Each element consists of two of these primary qualities, one active and the other passive. The element of fire comprises the primary qualities of hot and dry. Heat, the active quality renders fire expansive; dryness, the passive quality, adds a lack of adaptability. Therefore, the element of fire imposes its nature onto things, it causes change without being changed itself. The element of air comprises the primary qualities of hot and moist. The union of these two primary qualities suggests that the element of air is as dynamic as the element of fire, but through its inherent moisture it becomes more adaptable. Because fire and air share the hot quality, they are both seen as dynamic, masculine and extrovert. Opposed to these, the element of earth comprises the primary qualities of cold and dry. Cold, the active quality makes the element of earth contracting and inert. Dryness, the passive quality, renders it hard and unable to mould itself onto anything. The fourth element, water, comprises the primary qualities of cold and moist. As in the case of the element of earth, the active quality of cold makes the element receptive and dense, but the passive quality of moist makes it very malleable. As earth and water share the cold quality, they are seen as feminine and introvert. The four elements can also be found in the human body wherein they are made manifest in the form of the four temperaments.

The Four Temperaments

Associated with the four elements of fire, earth, air and water, the four temperaments are found in each human being. The temperaments are *choleric, melancholic, sanguine* and *phlegmatic*. These four temperaments define what is called the *complexion* of each individual. Each temperament has associated with it certain psychological predispositions, behavioural patterns and a specific physical structure, including the so-called *humour*. These four humours are called *yellow bile, black bile, blood* and *phlegm*. Each individual usually shows one predominant temperament, although the other three will be present to some degree and add to the overall picture.

Choleric

The choleric temperament combines the primary qualities of hot and dry and is associated with the element of fire. People whose temperament is mainly choleric are enthusiastic, optimistic, assertive, and often aggressive. They are always ready for action, are enterprising and enthusiastic, often impatient. Typically, cholerics have a tendency to change their minds and will work on a number of projects at once. Because cholerics are primarily hot and dry, they may not experience deep emotions very often. The body of the choleric tends to be muscular but slim, although this might be slightly modified by the presence of other temperaments. The choleric temperament is associated with the humour of *yellow bile*. According to traditional teachings, this humour, located in the gall bladder, processes the other three humours and is thought to heat up the body.

Melancholic

The melancholic temperament consists of the primary qualities of cold and dry and is associated with the element of earth. Typical melancholics are analytical, studious people who can be very unsociable. Appearing to be reserved, they can easily be underestimated or overlooked. Melancholics are generally very patient, but their rigidity, due to the cold quality, can make them pessimistic, melancholic and even depressed. Due to the dry quality they may become intolerant and resentful which in turn can lead to separation and loneliness. The body of the melancholic is slim, with a medium frame, although this might differ slightly, due to the presence of other temperaments. The melancholic temperament is connected with the humour called *black bile* that is thought to reside in the spleen and is responsible for the retention of substances in the human body.

Sanguine

The sanguine temperament combines the primary qualities of hot and moist and is associated with the element of air. Sanguines are generally friendly, happy people who can be very sensitive. One typical characteristic of the sanguine temperament is a lack of concentration and very often they lack of persistence or perseverance. They can seem to be quite unsettled and restless and may therefore appear superficial. The body of the sanguine is of medium height and they tend to be rather on the full side. As indicated by its Latin name, the sanguine temperament is connected with the humour called *blood*. This humour is responsible for the transport of substances through the body via the veins and arteries as well as for the excretion of certain substances.

Phlegmatic

The phlegmatic temperament consists of the primary qualities of cold and moist and is associated with the element of water. People whose temperament is mainly phlegmatic are sensitive, emotional people with a strong emotional emphasis. They are generally introverted, but unlike people of the melancholic temperament, they show a high level of adaptability and flexibility. Although both the phlegmatic and the melancholic temperament share the primary quality of cold, the phlegmatic has moisture instead of the melancholic's dryness. By emphasising their emotional side, phlegmatics tend to be quite inconsistent and can appear to be subjective. Sometimes there can also be found an element of laziness. The body of the phlegmatic tends to be rather short and there is a distinct possibility of weight gain throughout life. This temperament is connected with the humour called *phlegm,* responsible for the constant regulation and maintenance of the body's temperature.

Various methods have been used throughout history to establish a person's temperament. In this book I will focus largely on one particular method, adding a few details that have validated themselves in my practical work through increased accuracy. This way of establishing a person's temperament was first described in Ferdinand Rensberger's astrological textbook *Astronomia Teutsch*, published at Augsburg in 1569. In the chapter *Of the Complexions*, one can find a detailed description and an example of judging the temperament of a nativity. According to Rensberger, the following points need to be tabulated before a person's temperament can be established:

1.   the rising sign;

2.   its Lord;

3.   the sign the Moon is in;

4.   its Lord;

5.   the phase of the Moon;

6.   quarta anni solis;

7.   the sign the Sun is in;

8.   its Lord;

9.   the Lord of Birth.

1. The Rising Sign

The rising sign is the sign on the Ascendant or first house cusp of the birth chart in question.

Aries, Leo, Sagittarius are hot and dry, choleric;

Taurus, Virgo, Capricorn are cold and dry, melancholic;

Gemini, Libra, Aquarius are warm and moist, sanguine;

Cancer, Scorpio, Pisces are cold and moist, phlegmatic.

2. Its Lord

This is the ruler of the sign on the Ascendant or first house cusp.

Aries and Scorpio are ruled by Mars;

Taurus and Libra are ruled by Venus;

Gemini and Virgo are ruled by Mercury;

Cancer is ruled by the Moon;

Leo is ruled by the Sun;

Sagittarius and Pisces are ruled by Jupiter;

Capricorn and Aquarius are ruled by Saturn.

The qualities of the planets are as follows:

Saturn, cold and dry, melancholic;

Jupiter, warm and moist, sanguine;

Mars, hot and dry, choleric;

Venus, cold and moist, phlegmatic;

Mercury by himself is hot and dry, but when he is with other planets that are hot and dry or warm and moist, he will help to increase their qualities. Likewise with those planets that are cold and dry or cold and moist. Mercury changes his nature according to the quality of the twelve heavenly signs: in cold signs he is cold; in warm or hot signs, hot; in moist signs, moist. Mercury transforms his nature according to the planet or sign he comes to because he is a helper and therefore he helps evil when with the evil and good when with the good. The Dragon's Head acts in the same way increasing the good when with the good and the evil when with the evil. But the Dragon's Tail decreases evil in the evil and decreases good in the good. Everyone who wants to achieve something in this art should notice this difference.

3. The Sign the Moon is in
Aries, Leo, Sagittarius are hot and dry, choleric;

Taurus, Virgo, Capricorn are cold and dry, melancholic;

Gemini, Libra, Aquarius are warm and moist, sanguine;

Cancer, Scorpio, Pisces are cold and moist, phlegmatic.

4. Its Lord

The planetary ruler of the sign in which the Moon is placed. (For rulership and qualities, see point 2.)

5. The Phase of the Moon

From New Moon to First Quarter is warm and moist;

From First Quarter to Full is hot and dry;

From Full to Last Quarter is cold and dry;

From Last Quarter to New Moon is cold and moist.

6. Quarta Anni Solis

Here we must establish in which quarter of the year the Sun was at time of birth. The quarters of the year are equivalent to the four seasons. When the Sun is in Aries, Taurus or Gemini it is springtime and like the spring, he is seen as hot and moist. But when the Sun is in Cancer, Leo or Virgo, the summer, he is hot and dry. When the Sun is in Libra, Scorpio or Sagittarius it is autumn and he is cold and dry. When the Sun is in Capricorn, Aquarius or Pisces, like the winter he is cold and moist.

7. The Sign the Sun is in

Aries, Leo, Sagittarius are hot and dry, choleric;

Taurus, Virgo, Capricorn are cold and dry, melancholic;

Gemini, Libra, Aquarius are warm and moist, sanguine;

Cancer, Scorpio, Pisces are cold and moist, phlegmatic.

8. Its Lord

The planetary ruler of the sign the Sun is in. (For rulership and qualities, see point 2.)

9. The Lord of Birth

The Lord of Birth, also known as the Lord of the Geniture, is the overall ruler of the chart. Throughout history, the techniques that were used to establish the Lord or Lady of the Geniture have changed: for example, Ferdinand Rensberger used the five hylegiacal places, namely Sun, Moon, Ascendant, Part of Fortune, and the degree of the conjunction or prevention which has taken place before birth (the pre-natal syzygy). He proposed that the planet with the most essential dignity in these five places would be the Lord of the Geniture. Although this is a very complex technique, it does not take into account how much a planet is enabled to act which is expressed through its accidental dignities or debilities (this will be explained in great detail in the chapter *Dignities and Debilities*). For this reason, I decided to use the method William Lilly recommends in *Christian Astrology*. He writes that the planet that has most essential and accidental dignities in the birth chart, is in the best position and most elevated, should be the Lord of the Geniture.

To emphasise the importance of the rising sign, the Moon's sign and the quarta anni solis, we allocate two points to them. All the other factors are represented by one point. The following table shows a summary of the different attributes allocated to each of the four temperaments.

	Sanguine	Choleric	Melancholic	Phlegmatic
	(hot & moist)	(hot & dry)	(cold & dry)	(cold & moist)
Element	Air	Fire	Earth	Water
Sign	♊ ♎ ♒	♈ ♌ ♐	♉ ♍ ♑	♋ ♏ ♓
Planet	♃ ♀ (oriental) ♀ (oriental)	☉ ♂	♄ ♀ (occidental)	☽ ♀ (occidental)
Phase of the Moon	New to First Quarter	First Quarter to Full	Full to Last Quarter	Last Quarter to New
Quarta Anni Solis	Sun in ♈ ♉ ♊	Sun in ♋ ♌ ♍	Sun in ♎ ♏ ♐	Sun in ♑ ♒ ♓
Season	Spring	Summer	Autumn	Winter

Traditionally, all astrologers agree that the Sun, Moon, Mars, Jupiter and Saturn have certain intrinsic qualities and therefore each of those planets can be allocated to one particular temperament. This is not the case with Venus and Mercury. Although it is generally agreed that Venus is moist, astrological practitioners have long debated if she should be hot or cold. The answer may lie in the fact that as the Lesser Benefic she is generally temperate and is therefore able to warm up cold things and cool down hot ones. There is a similar issue with Mercury, who is seen as hot, cold, moist or dry thus 'changeable'. To solve this problem, I have adopted the solution the astrologer and scholar Dorian Gieseler Greenbaum suggests in her book *Temperament, Astrology's Forgotten Key*. She suggests allocating the primary qualities hot and moist to Venus and Mercury in oriental position. If Venus is positioned occidentally she is cold and moist and if Mercury is occidental, he is cold and dry. A planet is said to be oriental when rising before the Sun and occidental when rising after the Sun.

In the following, the nativity of Marsilio Ficino is used as an example of how to establish a person's temperament from their birth chart.

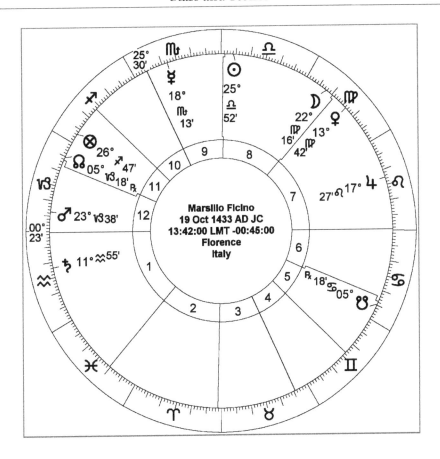

Marsilio Ficino was an important Renaissance philosopher and astrologer. He translated some of Plato's works from Greek into Latin, and by so doing revived Neo-Platonism. Ficino was a self-confessed melancholic, which is corroborated by our own findings about his temperament.

		Sanguine	Choleric	Melancholic	Phlegmatic
Rising Sign	♒	2			
Its Lord	♄			1	
Moon Sign	♑			2	
Its Lord	♑			1	
Moon Phase	4/4				1
QAS	Autumn			2	
Sun Sign	♏				1
Its Lord	♂		1		
LoG	♄			1	
Score		2	1	7	2

The Planets

Natural Significations, Rulerships and Properties

Saturn

Saturn is a diurnal, masculine planet, and is cold and dry. He is associated with the element of earth and the melancholic temperament. Being the slowest and the most distant of the seven traditional planets it takes Saturn about twenty-nine and a half years to complete one of his cycles. In other words, he spends about two and a half years in each zodiacal sign. This is the reason that he represents limitation, isolation and austerity. The slowness of motion also makes him a significator of time, maturity, old age, decline and death. Saturn is known as the *Greater Malefic*, or the *Greater Infortune*, connected with fear, envy and hatred. The Arab astrologer al-Biruni calls him "disagreeable and astringent, offensively acid and stinking". Illnesses associated with Saturn are problems with the right ear, pains in limbs and joints, rheumatism, gout, fractures, problems with the teeth, such as loose or irregular teeth and rotten gums.

Jupiter

Jupiter is a diurnal, masculine planet, and he is moderately hot and moist. He is associated with the element of air and the sanguine temperament. It takes Jupiter a little under twelve years to complete one of his cycles; this means that he passes through one zodiacal sign per year. His brightness and high visibility, which is only surpassed by Venus, make Jupiter a symbol of harmony, justice, kindness and charity. He is also known as the *Greater Benefic*, or the *Greater Fortune*. Well-dignified he represents faith, honour and godliness, making him full of charity, a lover of fair dealing and a reliever of the poor. Jupiter also signifies temperance, sobriety and modesty. William Lilly tells us that Jupiter "gives good luck in sciences such as the law or religion or perhaps through being made a bishop or judge". Illnesses associated with Jupiter are problems with the left ear, inflammation of the lungs, all blood related diseases, liver problems, heart palpitations, back problems, convulsions, and cramps.

Mercury

Mercury is a neutral planet and he can be masculine or feminine, according to his position and aspects. Some authors state that he has a dry nature when isolated from the other planets. He is the closest planet to the Sun and can never be more than 27 degrees away from him. For this reason, he can only aspect the Sun by conjunction but never by sextile, trine, square or opposition. Mercury can move very fast and it is possible for him to spend only three weeks in one zodiacal sign. Due to his variable condition and potential speed, he signifies communication, commerce, transport and trade. Mercury also represents writing, education, language and intellectual activities in general. Well-dignified, Mercury signifies scholarly, often logical people, but also travellers and merchants. When ill-dignified, he signifies liars, cheats and people with no substantial education, a disorganised mind, or even downright fools. Illnesses associated with Mercury are diseases of the brain, vertigo, stammering, speech defects, an overactive imagination, dumbness and memory loss. Hiebner also lists lethargy, madness, and hoarseness as illnesses corresponding to Mercury.

Mars

Mars is a nocturnal, masculine planet, and he is excessively hot and dry. He is associated with the fire element and the choleric temperament. He is the first of the superior planets with his orbit outside that of the Earth and for this reason he can cast any aspect to the Sun. Mars spends about two months in each zodiacal sign. Due to his nature, swiftness and his characteristically red colour, he is associated with fire and war. Mars is also known as the *Lesser Malefic* or *Lesser Infortune*. Well-dignified, Mars represents bold and confident people, invincible in feats of war and courageous, but when ill-dignified he signifies lovers of slaughter and violence, thieves, traitors, immodest, unthankful people and cheats. Illnesses associated with Mars are fevers, migraines, blisters, wounds particularly from iron, scars, stones and diseases in men's genitals.

Venus

Venus is a nocturnal, feminine planet, and she is hot and moist (or cold and moist, according to some authors, as explained in the chapter on temperaments). She is associated with the element of air and water and the sanguine and phlegmatic temperaments. Venus is positioned between the Sun and the Earth and therefore cannot be further away from the Sun than 48 degrees. In other words, she can only aspect the Sun by conjunction but never by sextile, trine, square or opposition. Venus spends approximately four weeks in each zodiacal sign. She is also known as the *Lesser Benefic* or the *Lesser Fortune*. Venus is the brightest planet in the sky and William Lilly says that Venus "is well known amongst the vulgar by the name of evening Starre or *Hesperus*" when appearing after sunset, but "common people call her the morning Starre, and the learned *Lucifer*" when visible before sunrise. Venus signifies grace and beauty, softness, friendship, love in the carnal as well as the conceptual sense, passion and sexuality. Well-dignified she signifies serenity, cleanliness, cheerfulness and joy, but when ill-dignified Venus represents laziness, adultery, extravagance and carelessness. Illnesses associated with Venus are problems with the stomach, sexually transmitted diseases, impotence, diabetes, hernias and diseases of the kidneys, loins and genitals.

Sun

The Sun, also known as *Oculus Mundi*, the Eye of the World or *Fons Lucis*, the Fountain of Light, is diurnal, masculine and his nature is moderately hot and dry. He is associated with the fire element, but contrary to Mars, this fire is not destructive, but warming and illuminating. Well-dignified, the Sun is seen as equivalent to the Fortunes, full of fidelity and kept promises, but when ill-dignified he signifies vulgarity, arrogance, snobbery and foolishness. Illnesses associated with the Sun are fevers, palpitations, diseases of the heart or brain, cramps, weakness of sight and fainting.

Moon

The Moon, also known as the Lady of the Night or the Lesser Luminary, is a nocturnal, feminine planet, cold and moist. She is the only astrological planet that does not orbit the Sun. During her cycle of movement around the Earth, which is completed every twenty-nine and a half days, she perfects different aspects to the Sun, also known as the phases of the Moon. Being closely connected to the Greater Luminary and reflecting his light, the Moon symbolises organic life and the cyclical process of birth, life and death. This symbolism is also often connected with the phases of the Moon, whereby the New Moon is associated with birth, the waxing phase with growth, the Full Moon with maturity but also the turning point, the waning phase with decline and the Dark Moon with death. Well-dignified, the Moon indicates soft, peace-loving people, tender, honest and free from life's cares, but when ill-dignified she signifies idle and careless people who lack spirit and dislike work. Illnesses associated with the Moon are rheumatism, bowel problems, disorders of the eyes, stomach, bladder or liver, lunacy and vertigo. Hiebner also lists ulcers, measles, and epilepsy as illnesses corresponding to the Moon.

The Signs of the Zodiac

General Description of the Signs

Aries

The first sign of the zodiac, Aries, is fiery, hot and dry. The corresponding temperament is that of the choleric. This sign belongs to the fire triplicity and is masculine. Aries' mode is moveable (cardinal). It is the diurnal house of Mars and 19 degrees Aries is the place of the Sun's exaltation. Diseases associated with Aries are headaches, pimples in the face, polyps, ringworms and toothache.

Taurus

The second sign of the zodiac, Taurus, is earthy, cold and dry. The corresponding temperament is that of the melancholic. This sign belongs to the earth triplicity and is feminine. Taurus' mode is fixed. It is the nocturnal house of Venus and 3 degrees Taurus is the place of the Moon's exaltation. Diseases associated with Taurus are a sore throat, scrofula, tonsillitis, tuberculosis and benign skin tumours.

Gemini

The third sign of the zodiac, Gemini, is airy, hot and moist. The corresponding temperament is that of the sanguine. This sign belongs to the air triplicity and is masculine. Gemini's mode is mutable. It is the diurnal house of Mercury. Diseases associated with Gemini are bad blood and problems with the hands, arms and shoulders.

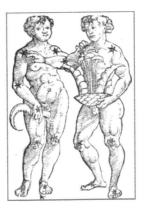

Cancer

The fourth sign of the zodiac, Cancer, is watery, cold and moist. The corresponding temperament is that of the phlegmatic. This sign belongs to the water triplicity and is feminine. Its mode is moveable. It is the only house of the Moon and 15 degrees Cancer is the place of Jupiter's exaltation. Diseases associated with Cancer are breast problems, coughs, stomach problems and weak digestion.

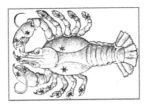

Leo

The fifth sign of the zodiac, Leo, is fiery, hot and dry. The corresponding temperament is that of the choleric. This sign belongs to the fire triplicity and is masculine. Its mode is fixed and it is the only house of the Sun. Diseases associated with Leo are back pains, eye problems, fevers and heart problems.

Virgo

The sixth sign of the zodiac, Virgo, is earthy, cold and dry. The corresponding temperament is that of the melancholic. This sign belongs to the earth triplicity and is feminine. Its mode is mutable. It is the nocturnal house of Mercury and 15 degrees is the place of Mercury's exaltation. Diseases associated with Virgo are colic, diseases of the belly, obstruction of the bowels and winds.

Libra

The seventh sign of the zodiac, Libra, is airy, hot and moist. The corresponding temperament is that of the sanguine. This sign belongs to the air triplicity and is masculine. Its mode is moveable. It is the diurnal house of Venus and 21 degrees Libra is the place of Saturn's exaltation. Diseases associated with Libra are corruption of the blood, kidney stones and ulcers.

Scorpio

The eighth sign of the zodiac, Scorpio, is watery, cold and moist. The corresponding temperament is that of the phlegmatic. This sign belongs to the water triplicity and is feminine. Its mode is fixed. It is the house of Mars. Diseases associated with Scorpio are afflictions of the genitals, bladder problems and stones.

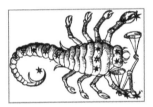

Sagittarius

The ninth sign of the zodiac, Sagittarius, is fiery, hot and dry. The corresponding temperament is that of the choleric. This sign belongs to the fire triplicity and is masculine. Its mode is mutable. It is the diurnal house of Jupiter. Diseases associated with Sagittarius are falls, fevers, injuries caused by fire or heat and wounds to the thighs or buttocks.

Capricorn

The tenth sign of the zodiac, Capricorn, is earthy, cold and dry. The corresponding temperament is that of the melancholic. This sign belongs to the earth triplicity and is feminine. Its mode is moveable. It is the nocturnal house of Saturn and 28 degrees Capricorn is the place of Mars' exaltation. Diseases associated with Capricorn are knee problems, itches and scabs.

Aquarius

The eleventh sign of the zodiac, Aquarius, is airy, hot and moist. The corresponding temperament is that of the sanguine. This sign belongs to the air triplicity and is masculine. Its mode is fixed. It is the diurnal house of Saturn. Diseases associated with Aquarius are blood clots, cramps and illnesses connected with the legs.

Pisces

The twelfth sign of the zodiac, Pisces, is watery, cold and moist. The corresponding temperament is that of the phlegmatic. This sign belongs to the water triplicity and is feminine. Its mode is mutable. It is the nocturnal house of Jupiter and 27 degrees Scorpio is the place of Venus' exaltation. Diseases associated with Pisces are colds, boils, and diseases of the feet, gout, lameness and ulcers.

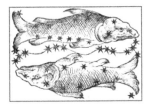

&co&

Signs and Elements:

Fire: Aries, Leo, and Sagittarius

Earth: Taurus, Virgo, and Capricorn

Air: Gemini, Libra, and Aquarius

Water: Cancer, Scorpio, and Pisces

&co&

Signs and Modes:

Moveable: Aries, Cancer, Libra, and Capricorn

Fixed: Taurus, Leo, Scorpio, and Aquarius

Mutable: Gemini, Virgo, Sagittarius, and Pisces

&co&

Signs and Parts of the Body:

Aries: head and face;

Taurus: neck and throat;

Gemini: hands, arms, shoulders;

Cancer: breast, ribs, stomach, spleen;

Leo: heart, back, spinal column;

Virgo: intestines, diaphragm;

Libra: lower back, kidneys, bladder, and urinary system;

Scorpio: genitals, anus;

Sagittarius: thighs and buttocks;

Capricorn: knees;

Aquarius: legs and ankles;

Pisces: feet.

જેન્

The Houses

First House

The first house is angular and masculine; in times past it was also called the 'horoscope'. It generally signifies a person's individuality and is the house of life, signifying the vitality and general physical appearance of the native. In the body, the first house represents the head and face. Its co-significators are Aries and Saturn. Venus and Jupiter in the first house give the best complexion, Mercury and Moon the next best. A placement of the Greater and Lesser Malefics, Saturn or Mars, can cause "ill faces or complexions", according to William Lilly.

Second House

The second house is succedent and feminine. It signifies resources and assets, representing the native's possible wealth or poverty. It also signifies moveable possessions. In the body the second house represents the native's throat, neck and shoulders. Its co-significators are Taurus and Jupiter. If Jupiter, the Greater Benefic, is ruler of the second house or is placed therein, it signifies wealth. If either Mars or the Sun is placed in this house, it indicates loss of money or a decrease of wealth.

Third House

The third house is cadent and masculine. It signifies the native's brothers, sisters and close relatives. It also represents "short journeys, or inland-journeys, oft removing from one place to another, epistles, letters, rumours and messengers", according to William Lilly. In the body the third house represents shoulders, arms, hands and fingers. Its co-significators are Gemini and Mars. Placed in this house, Mars is not seen as unfortunate unless in conjunction with Saturn.

Fourth House

The fourth house is angular and feminine; it is also known as *Imum Coeli*. It signifies ancestral roots, parents in general, but particularly the native's father. It represents assets and possessions, which are immoveable, like property or land (in contrast to money, which is signified by the second house) and resources acquired through inheritance. In the body, the fourth house signifies breast, chest and lungs. Its co-significators are Cancer and the Sun. If the Sun is placed here, the native's father is of "noble disposition", according to William Lilly.

Fifth House

The fifth house is succedent and masculine. It signifies playful activities, entertainment, love, sex and pleasure. For this reason it also represents fertility, the condition of a pregnant woman and the native's children. In the body, the fifth house signifies the stomach, heart and liver, sides and back. Its co-significators are Leo and Venus. If either Saturn or Mars is placed here and not particularly well dignified, this placement may be unfortunate. If Jupiter is placed in the fifth house it is a strong indicator for pregnancy.

Sixth House

The sixth house is cadent and feminine. It signifies the cause of illness and whether it is curable or incurable. William Lilly wrote in *Christian Astrology* that it signifies men, maidservants and galley slaves, day labourers, tenants and farmers. In the body it signifies the intestines and the back down to the backside. Its co-significators are Virgo and Mercury.

Seventh House

The seventh house is angular and masculine. It represents the 'significant other' in partnerships and relationships because of its opposition to the first house. The significant other can be a spouse in a romantic relationship, but may also be a business partner. The seventh house can signify opponents, open enemies or thieves. In the body, it signifies the area between the navel and the thighs. Its co-significators are Libra and the Moon. If either Saturn or Mars is placed in the seventh house, it is seen as unfortunate.

Eighth House

The eighth house is succedent and feminine. It signifies death, loss, wills, legacies, and inheritances. This house also represents fear and anguish. In the body, the eighth house signifies the genitals, bladder, stones, and poisons. Its co-significators are Scorpio and Saturn.

Ninth House

The ninth house is cadent and masculine. It signifies long journeys, formerly called 'travels by sea'. It also represents faith and religion, education, dreams, visions, and prophecy. In the body, the ninth house signifies the hips and thighs. Its co-significators are Sagittarius and Jupiter. If Jupiter is placed here, it indicates a devout person.

Tenth House

The tenth house is angular and feminine; it is also called *Medium Coeli* or midheaven. It signifies temporal power, figures of authority, vocation, career and profession. It also represents the native's mother. In the body, the tenth house represents the knees. Its co-significators are Capricorn and Mars. If either Jupiter or the Sun is placed in this house, it is seen as fortunate. Saturn or the Moon's south node, on the other hand, tends to signify a lack of achievements or honours.

Eleventh House

The eleventh house is succedent and masculine. It signifies friends and allies, help, support, reassurance, and trust. It is also the house of hopes and wishes, dreams and expectations. In the body the eleventh house represents the legs down to the ankles. Its co-significators are Aquarius and the Sun. It is seen as the greatest benefit if Jupiter is placed in this house.

Twelfth House

The twelfth house is cadent and feminine. It signifies prisons, enclosures, secret or hidden enemies, sorrow, envy, betrayal, affliction and self-undoing. In the body the twelfth house also represents the feet. Its co-rulers are Pisces and Venus.

ॐ

Dignities and Debilities

Sign	Ruler	Exal-tation	Triplicity Day Night	Term	Face	Detri-ment	Fall							
♈	♂	☉ 19	☉	♃	♃ 6	♀ 14	☿ 21	♂ 26	♄ 30	♂ 10	☉ 20	♀ 30	♀	♄
♉	♀	☽ 3	♀	☽	♀ 8	☿ 15	♃ 22	♄ 26	♂ 30	☿ 10	☽ 20	♄ 30	♂	
♊	☿		♄	☿	☿ 7	♃ 14	♀ 21	♄ 25	♂ 30	♃ 10	♂ 20	☉ 30	♃	
♋	☽	♃ 15	♂	♂	♂ 6	♃ 13	☿ 20	♀ 27	♄ 30	♀ 10	☿ 20	☽ 30	♄	♂
♌	☉		☉	♃	♄ 6	☿ 13	♀ 19	♃ 25	♂ 30	♄ 10	♃ 20	♂ 30	♄	
♍	☿	☿ 15	♀	☽	☿ 7	♀ 13	♃ 18	♄ 24	♂ 30	☉ 10	♀ 20	☿ 30	♃	♀
♎	♀	♄ 21	♄	☿	♄ 6	♀ 11	♃ 19	☿ 24	♂ 30	☽ 10	♄ 20	♃ 30	♂	☉
♏	♂		♂	♂	♂ 6	♃ 14	♀ 21	☿ 27	♄ 30	♂ 10	☉ 20	♀ 30	♀	☽
♐	♃		☉	♃	♃ 8	♀ 14	☿ 19	♄ 25	♂ 30	☿ 10	☽ 20	♄ 30	☿	
♑	♄	♂ 28	♀	☽	♀ 6	☿ 12	♃ 19	♂ 25	♄ 30	♃ 10	♂ 20	☉ 30	☽	
♒	♄		♄	☿	♄ 6	☿ 12	♀ 20	♃ 25	♂ 30	♀ 10	☿ 20	☽ 30	☉	
♓	♃	♀ 27	♂	♂	♀ 8	♃ 14	☿ 20	♂ 26	♄ 30	♄ 10	♃ 20	♂ 30	☿	☿

By assessing the level of essential dignity for each planet, the astrologer tries to establish how much of its essence, or its individual part of the divine light, is available at a particular moment in time. Such information improves the accuracy of the astrological judgement.

Essential Dignities

Lilly's essential dignities, as given in his *Christian Astrology*:

Essential Dignities		Essential Debilities	
A planet in his domicile (or mutual reception between domiciles)	5	In his detriment	-5
In his exaltation (or reception between exaltations)	4	In his fall	-4
In his own triplicity	3	Peregrine	-5
In his own term	2		
Decanate or face	1		

Accidental Dignities

Lilly's accidental dignities and debilities, as given in his *Christian Astrology*:

Accidental Dignities		Accidental Debilities	
In the midheaven or ascendant	5	In the 12th house	-5
In the 7th, 4th or 11th house	4	In the 8th and 6th house	-2
In the 2nd and 5th	3		
In the 9th	2		
In the 3rd house	1		
Direct (the ☉ and ☽ are always direct)	4	Retrograde	-5
Swift in motion	2	Slow in motion	-2
♄ ♃ ♂ when oriental	2	♄ ♃ ♂ occidental	-2
☿ and ♀ when occidental	2	☿ and ♀ oriental	-2
☽ increasing, or when occidental	2	☽ decreasing in light	-2
Free from combustion and sunbeams	5	Combust of the ☉	-5
In the heart of the ☉, or cazimi	5	Under the sunbeams	-4
In partile conjunction with ♃ and ♀	5	Partile conjunction with ♄ or ♂	-5
In partile conjunction with ☊	4	Partile conjunction with ☋	-4
In partile trine with ♃ and ♀	4	Besieged between ♄ and ♂	-5
In partile sextile with ♃ and ♀	3	Partile opposition with ♄ or ♂	-4
In conjunction with Cor Leonis	6	Partile square with ♄ or ♂	-3
In conjunction with Spica	5	In conjunction with Caput Algol	-5

PART TWO –

PLANETS AND GEMSTONES

Such is the power of the heavens in well-disposed material, such the swiftness. (Marsilio Ficino)

Since the dawn of time, gemstones and crystals have fascinated humans, by their mysterious sparkle, their beautiful colours and their intriguing shapes and symmetries. People collected them and even added them to the grave goods placed next to their loved ones, making sure that they would be able to use these precious stones in their next life. Although we do not know exactly when people first became aware of them, it is likely that the healing properties of crystals and gemstones have been known for millennia. In the 3rd century AD, the prominent Greek physician Galen wrote about the medicinal uses of stones. Later, in the 12th century, Abbess Hildegard of Bingen included a book on the healing properties of gemstones in her important work, *Physica*. At about the same time, the distinguished Jewish writer and astrologer Abraham ibn Ezra published tables showing the connection between planets and gemstones. Then 400 years later, in 1533, Heinrich Cornelius Agrippa von Nettesheim published his ground-breaking compilation *De Occulta Philosophia Libri Tres*. In this work, Agrippa dedicates a whole chapter to the correspondences between metals, gemstones, herbs and the seven planets. It has to be noted that astrologers had already recorded these correspondences at least 1000 years earlier. Al Biruni's *Book of the Instructions in the Elements of the Art of Astrology*, first published in 1029, lists them. Although the knowledge of these correspondences is almost forgotten now, we have to realise that in centuries past educated people were very much aware of these ideas. As well as corresponding to particular crystals or gemstones, each of the seven planets also corresponded to one of the seven metals. The great English poet of the 14th century, Geoffrey Chaucer, wrote about these correspondences in his *Canterbury Tales*:

"The bodies sevene eek lo! hem heer anoon: Sol gold is, and Luna silver we thrape, Mars yren, Mercurie quick-silver we clepe, Saturnus leed, and Jupiter is tin, And Venus coper, by my fader kin."

Chaucer knew that Mars and iron, Sun and gold, Moon and silver, Mercury and quicksilver, Venus and copper, Jupiter and tin, and Saturn and lead were connected.

We cannot know for certain how the old masters found out about the inherent nature of metals, revealing the corresponding colour, but modern technology seems to prove that their findings were correct.

The table below shows the wavelengths of colour throughout the visible spectrum.

Red	750nm - 620nm
Orange	620nm – 590nm
Yellow	590nm – 570nm
Green	570nm – 495nm
Blue	495nm – 450nm
Violet	450nm – 380nm

Everything emits light when heated and this is also the case for each of the seven metals we are particularly interested in. When sent through a spectroscope, the light of each metal produces a unique spectrum of frequencies of electromagnetic radiation, also known as emission spectrum. Each emission spectrum appears in a series of lines, called the line spectrum. A close investigation of each metal's line spectrum shows that its first lines or rays are in correspondence with the colour attributed to the corresponding planet. Using this information, we can now move one step further and deduce that the correspondences between planets and colours are correct. If, for example, we look at the emission spectrum of tin, we find that its first spectral ray falls into the zone of dark blue and indigo, at around 450nm. We also know that, as seen in Chaucer's quote above, Jupiter is the planet traditionally associated with tin. Therefore we can logically deduce that if it is true that the corresponding colour of tin is dark blue or indigo, it must also be true that it is the corresponding colour of Jupiter. This also ties in with the Neo-Platonic concept known as the 'great chain of being', which will be discussed in Chapter 3.

As one of the most significant elements of magical symbolism, these planetary colour correspondences have been known for millennia. Detailed information about them can be found in the writings of the Hermetic Order of the Golden Dawn. Although this is not the place to delve deeply into the mysteries of the Golden Dawn, the Tree of Life, or the secrets of ceremonial magic, I want to draw attention to the Order's four scales of colour. The cabbalistic Tree of Life is thought to exist simultaneously in the Archetypal World (Aziluth), the World of Creation (Briah), the World of Formation (Yetzirah), and the Material World (Assiah). These four Worlds may be thought of as different levels of the manifestation of the Divine. Each of the Tree's 10 spheres and 22 paths manifests a specific vibration in each of the four worlds. We are only concerned with the correspondences between Sephirot, planets and colours in Assiah, the material world, which is also known as the 'Princess scale'. The following is a tabulated excerpt from *Ritual "W" Hodos – Chamelionis*:

| Sephira | Princess Scale | |
	Colour	Planet
Binah	Grey flecked pink	Saturn
Chesed	Deep azure flecked yellow	Jupiter
Geburah	Red flecked black	Mars
Tipareth	Gold amber	Sun
Netzach	Olive flecked gold	Venus
Hod	Yellow-brown flecked white	Mercury
Yesod	Citrine flecked azure	Moon

A different approach, based on alchemical symbolism, may also help to shed more light on the vital importance of the correspondences.

Element	Colour	Planet
Fire	Red	Mars
Earth	Violet/dark blue	Jupiter
Air	White	Moon
Water	Blue	Venus
Sal	Black	Saturn
Sulphur	Orange	Sun
Mercury	Green	Mercury

René Schwaller de Lubicz, the man believed to have been behind the pseudonym of the legendary alchemist Fulcanelli, claimed that he recreated the blue stained glass, used in the windows of Chartres cathedral. The stained glass windows, which are perhaps the cathedral's most distinctive features, were made and installed at the beginning of the 13th century, but the process of creating the so-called Chartres-blue was lost or forgotten soon after. André VandenBroeck, a painter and writer, who for 18 months was in daily contact with de Lubicz, wrote extensively about their conversations in his book *Al-Kemi, A Memoir*. According to Vandenbroeck, Lubicz stated "The Chartres glass is dyed in its mass by the volatile spirit of metals". In other words, rather than any additive, it is the colour form of the metal itself, the imprint of the metallic soul, that creates the desired colour. What we should take from our short excursion into the realms of Kabbalah and alchemy is the realisation that the planets, metals and colours are not only in correspondence, but that they are in fact expressions of the same underlying principle. Therefore Mars is red, iron is red and Mars is iron, when seen from a non- linear perspective.

Iron / Red / Mars:

Iron's first spectral lines are to be found around the red zone of the spectrum at around 650nm. It is known that iron promotes the formation of haemoglobin in the body, and the functions of the liver, spleen and intestines are dependent upon the level of iron available. Healing practitioners are also convinced that, on the psychological level, iron has a stimulating effect, and also heightens levels of physical activity. Traditional astrological symbolism states that Mars has rulership over the blood. He is also significator of abscesses, dysentery, fevers, fistulas, hepatitis, rashes and wounds, particularly to the head and face.

Gold / Red - Orange / Sun:

The first two spectral rays of gold are to be found in the red and orange zones of the spectrum, at around 628nm and 595nm. On the physical level, gold helps the body to maintain circulation and it is responsible for the regulation of the impulses in the nervous system. It is believed that gold helps to combat depression and increases magnanimity and generosity. Traditional astrological symbolism states that the Sun has rulership over the nervous system, eyes and diseases of the eyes, the heart and heart diseases, and diseases of the mouth. Al-Biruni describes the Sun as the natural significator of generosity and the

17th century astrologer Claudius Dariot lists magnanimity as one of the Sun's correspondences.

Silver / Yellow (White) / Moon:

The spectral line of silver superimposes itself over the one of mercury (quicksilver) situated in the region of green and yellow, at around 570nm and 550nm. Silver is said to stimulate the bodily fluids, to increase sight and to help restoring one's balance. On a mental level, it helps to express one's feelings and also stimulates mental flexibility. Some spiritual practitioners claim that silver increases a person's psychic abilities. Traditional astrological symbolism connects the Moon with a person's mental problems. She is also the significator of epilepsy, lymph accumulation, obstructions, pregnancy, the skin and skin conditions, the stomach and stomach pains.

Mercury / Yellow - Green / Mercury:

The first spectral line of mercury is situated at the limit of green-yellow, at around 545nm. Mercury has no positive effects on the human body and any exposure to it in its elemental form should be avoided. Traditional astrological symbolism states that Mercury has rulership over the brain and diseases of the brain. He is also the significator of the ears, dumbness, hoarseness, imagination, madness, memory, tuberculosis, stammering, and vertigo.

Copper / Green - Blue / Venus:

Copper chloride contributes to the first band of the spectrum, two rays situated in the blue and blue-green zones, at around 530nm and 510 nm. The absorption of iron in the small intestines is promoted by copper and it also functions as a catalyst in the process of forming haemoglobin. Copper is well known to help with menstrual problems, is anti-inflammatory and it also stimulates the liver and brain. It is said that copper promotes love and friendship, and is responsible for our appreciation of beauty. Traditional astrological symbolism states that Venus has rulership over the liver and liver diseases. She also signifies the eyes and eyesight, women in general, and especially the female genitals, and the womb. There is also a connection to venereal diseases.

Tin / Blue - Indigo / Jupiter:

The spectral line of dichloride of tin falls precisely on the limits of dark blue and indigo, at around 450nm. Tin is thought to stimulate our brain activity, but it also has a positive influence on the nervous system. It is also said that tin can be beneficial when dealing with chronic problems, particularly problems of the respiratory tract. On a mental level, tin helps to increase tolerance and enthusiasm. Traditional astrological symbolism states that Jupiter has rulership over the lungs, lung diseases and inflammation of the lungs. He is also significator of asthma, fevers, the liver and inflammation of the liver, and pleurisy.

Lead / Violet (Black) / Saturn:

The spectrum of lead emits a ray in the first band in the middle of violet, at around 405nm. Lead is supposed to help with the body's detoxification, particularly the stomach and intestines. It also helps to prevent the formation of stones in organs. On a psychological level, lead helps against depression and seemingly unbearable restrictions. Traditional astrological symbolism states that Saturn has rulership over stones in the body, like gall- or kidney stones. He is also significator of bones, the bladder, consumption, jaundice, tertian fever (malaria), sciatica, and the spleen.

Saturn

Saturn's corresponding metal is lead and his corresponding colour is dark violet or black. He is a diurnal planet, masculine, cold and dry and governs the air triplicity, which comprises Gemini, Libra and Aquarius by day. Saturn is called the 'Greater Infortune' or 'Greater Malefic' due to his cold and dry nature and prolonged duration of affliction. Capricorn is his night house and Aquarius his day house. He is exalted in Libra and is in his fall in Aries. William Lilly writes in his *Christian Astrology* that Saturn's friends are Jupiter, Sun and Mercury, his enemies Mars and Venus. The actions of Saturn are generally binding, restricting and crystallising and he has hardening, limiting and depleting tendencies. He is associated with the melancholic temperament and the element of earth. Saturn is also a barren planet; women with an afflicted Saturn in the 5th house in their nativity may never give birth. Saturn rules bones, the skin and the right ear in the human body. Diseases of Saturn are coughs and cholics, deafness, oedema, impotency, sciatica, the swelling of tissue, toothache and weakness in the limbs. Saunders writes in his *Astrological Judgment of Physick* (1677) that Saturn in Sagittarius is indicative of a "contraction of the sinews". In the first 18 degrees of Taurus, he causes "visions and fantasies, melancholic passions, solitariness, heaviness and sadness". It also shows "stiffness of the limbs and sinews". Saturn is essentially debilitated if he is in his detriment, fall or peregrination. He also is accidentally debilitated if he is in house 6, 8 or 12; if he is retrograde, slow in motion, occidental, under the Sun's beams, combust, in partile conjunction with Cauda Draconis, partile conjunction with Mars, partile opposition with Mars or partile square with Mars, also if he is in conjunction with fixed star Caput Algol. (For a complete analysis of the dignities and debilities of the planets in a chart, see the diagram in Chapter 1). If Saturn is found to be generally afflicted in the birth chart or temporarily through transit or direction, two important gemstones can provide positive influence, these are jet and black onyx. Onyx of the red and white kind may be used in connection with Mars or Moon problems.

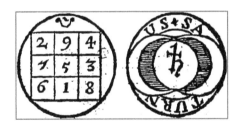

Jet (Gagates)

Jet is a light carbon fossil with a hardness of 2.5 to 4 and a specific gravity of 1.30 to 1.35. Pliny writes that

> "it is black, smooth, light and porous, differs but little from wood in appearance, is of brittle texture, and emits a disagreeable smell when rubbed."

It was formerly known as gagates, named after the city and river Gages in ancient Lycia, where it was first discovered. Another name for jet is 'black amber' because of its ability to acquire static electricity if friction is applied to its surface, just like real amber. Very often the two stones are found in the same beds of lignite, which suggests that amber and jet are nothing else but the fossilised branches and the fossilised resin of the same tree. At present it is found in the amber mines of the Baltic coast and in the United Kingdom, around Whitby, Yorkshire. Gagates has been used in Egypt for making mirrors, and the Romans valued jet for its medicinal qualities. They said that its fumes would drive away all sorts of reptiles and it could be useful against strangulations of the womb. It was also believed that it would restore menstruation. Later on, in medieval times, it was thought that its ingestion would serve as a cure for migraines; mixed with wine, jet could be taken for toothache and, when combined with beeswax, was applied as an ointment on tumours. In the 16th century, jet was a popular material for monks' and nuns' rosaries; it was believed that these beads would draw heavenly favours down onto the person using the rosary. It was also commonly applied to discover if a woman was still a virgin by adding powdered jet to water and drunk, after filtering, by the supposed virgin. If she was unable to urinate after ingestion of the water, she was still a virgin. Much loved as jewellery and used most extensively in Victorian times, gagates was known for its ability to bring grief to the surface, but it could also help to overcome it. John Maplet, the famous 16th century writer on natural philosophy, wrote about jet in his book *A Greene Forest, or a naturall Historie* (I have rectified the archaic spelling, random capitalisation and erratic punctuation of the original, making the quotes more palatable for the modern reader. I have tried, though, to preserve some of the style, so typical for 16th century publications):

> "Gagates is of the precious sort also, which was first found in Sicily in a certain place called Gagatus of the which it took his name: although that in Britain, it is a good guest & somewhat common as Isidore saith: It hath two kinds, the one russet in colour, and the other black, this last easy to be fired, and as smoky as frankincense. It being left in the place where serpents breed, drives them clean away. And Diascorides saith, that this being put into ye drink of a maid or virgin will easily give you judgement whether that she be a true and right maid yea or no.

For saith he, after that she hath drunk of this and does not a short time after make water, but can continue, than take her and esteem her a pure virgin, and contrariwise, if she doe not continue and stay herein some season, judge of her otherwise."

As a stone of protection, jet is used to guard against negativity and depression and to ease the pain associated with grieving and loss. It is also used to prevent sudden mood swings. Due to its organic nature, jet tends to dry out and may even crack if it is exposed to bright sunlight for prolonged periods of time.

কৈৎ

Onyx

There have been various and sometimes conflicting definitions of onyx throughout history and many ancient writers seem to make their own distinctions. Sometimes it was alabaster and sometimes marble that was called 'onyx'. Presently authors state that onyx, like sard and sardonyx, is a chalcedony, consisting of only two layers; one black and one white. Its black colour is due to the presence of iron and carbon. Sard is a brownish red variety of chalcedony, and sardonyx is a mixture between sard and onyx consisting of white and brown bands. Onyx has a Mohs hardness of 7 and a trigonal crystal structure. (For more on carnelian, sard, or sardonyx, see its entry under Mars stones.) John Maplet tells us about onyx in his *Greene Forest*:

> "Onyx of some onichus, is a stone of India and Arabia, having colours all about it intermeddled very like to a man's nail: whereupon the Greeks call our nail onikin. That of India hath a colour like to fire, & is dyed with white veins or zones. That of Arabia is black, yet died with white lines or zones. It hath many kinds of sardonix, so called for that by commixture of the onyx which is white and sardus which is red, it becometh but one of them both. It being borne about one, riddeth him of fear: and in manner of a glass it shows a man's visage, as says Diascorides."

In Greek, the word for fingernail is *onux* and there exists a Greek legend, telling the story of how onyx came to be so called. In this legend, Cupid, the god of love, was mischievously cutting the fingernails of his mother Venus, goddess of love and beauty, while she was asleep. He left the clippings scattered on the ground. The Moirae, goddesses who control everybody's destiny, turned the clippings into stone so that no part of Venus would ever perish. In medieval times, onyx was connected with bad luck and sadness, discord and egotism. Onyx was also used in dream-necromancy. If a person wanted to get into contact with a dead friend or relative, they were told to wear onyx set in a ring or a pendant during the night. After waking up the next morning, the wearer would be able to remember the conversation with the deceased. Today it is thought that onyx can boost a person's self-confidence. Those who are easily led and have problems making the right decisions will find that onyx helps them to find the right balance between sobriety and superficiality or facetiousness. In some cases the stone can have a grounding effect and will focus one's attention. Onyx can also increase analytical and logical thinking and may even improve the level of concentration. From a medicinal point of view, onyx can help to cure skin disorders, inflammations and fungal infections, boosting the immune system. It is also thought that onyx can help with diseases of the inner ear.

Jupiter

Jupiter's corresponding metal is tin and his corresponding colours are violet and purple. He is a diurnal planet, masculine, hot and moist and governs the fire triplicity comprising Aries, Leo and Sagittarius by night. Jupiter is called the Greater Fortune or Greater Benefic due to his ability to provide heat and moisture. Pisces is his night house and Sagittarius his day house. He is exalted in Cancer and is in his fall in Capricorn. He receives detriment in Gemini and Virgo. William Lilly writes in *Christian Astrology* that all planets, except Mars, are friends to Jupiter. This planet is positive, generous, kind in nature and rules over justice, moderation and temperance. He is associated with the element of air and also with the sanguine temperament. When well aspected, he is a preserver of life and can help to restore health. Jupiter rules over blood and blood circulation as well as births. Here particularly a positive direction to the Medium Coeli promises the birth of a child.

Furthermore he rules over the left ear, liver, and lungs. He is of a beneficent, conservative nature, moderate, preserving, religious and just. Afflictions of Jupiter can cause diseases of the liver, like a cold and dry liver, or inflammation; these afflictions may affect the blood, like blood poisoning, the lungs and indirectly the heart. Apoplexy, boils and cramps are also associated with Jupiter. If Jupiter is located between 7 and 24 degrees Libra, he "causes diseases of the blood", according to Saunders. In the last six degrees of Libra, he indicates "many diseases of blood in the liver and lungs". Jupiter is essentially debilitated if he is in his detriment, fall or peregrination. He is also accidentally debilitated if he is in house 6, 8 or 12, or when besieged between Saturn and Mars. (The complete tables of essential and accidental dignities and debilities may be consulted to find the degree of Jupiter's debility in any given chart.) If Jupiter is generally afflicted in a nativity, or temporarily debilitated through other influences, amethyst, lapis lazuli, sapphire, topaz or zircon may be used as remedies.

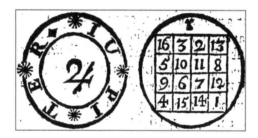

Amethyst

Amethyst has a Mohs hardness of seven and has a trigonal crystal structure. It belongs to the group of crystal quartzes; its colour is mainly due to the traces of iron it contains. An amethyst of high quality should have, when held up against the light and viewed sideways, a certain purple effulgence, slightly inclining towards a tint of rose. Stones of this high quality were often referred to as 'Venus' eyelid'. The name amethyst is derived from the Greek word *amethustos*, meaning 'not inebriated' or 'sober'. This may be due to its peculiar tint which has been described as very close to the colour of wine, but it may also be because of the stone's sobering and cleansing effects. The origin of the word 'amethyst', according to the Austrian Freiherr von Hammer Purgstall, could be found in the Persian word *chemest*. In 1818 Hammer Purgstall translated and published Mohammed Ben Mansur's *Book of Precious Stones*, originating from about 1300. In the book, Mansur repeats the ancient myth that "wine drunk out of a goblet of amethyst" would not intoxicate but implies the true origin of amethyst to be *chemest*. The 14th century writer Konrad von Megenberg says that amethyst "makes a person better, disperses bad thoughts, brings about good common sense and makes one mild and gentle". In 1567, John Maplet writes about the amethyst:

> "The amitist also groweth in India: It is princess among those gems that be purple coloured. Diascorides says, that there be five kinds thereof: but that which is purple coloured, he reckeneth the chiefest. His force or virtue availeth against drunkenness, it kepeth a man waking, and driveth away ill cogitations and thoughts, it sharpeneth the understanding. And is also one of those sorts that is easy to engrave in."

The Sanskrit name for amethyst is *cacunada*, bringer of luck. A Greek myth tells us that Diana, being jealous of a nymph called Ametis, who was preferred to her by Bacchus, transformed the nymph into a crystal. In a drunken rage, Bacchus poured wine over Ametis, turning her into an amethyst. This is where the name Bacchus-stone stems from. It is also an explanation for the inherent ability of the stone to prevent people from getting drunk. All of this shows the longstanding connectedness of amethysts and their beneficial effect on problems with the liver, which makes it an ideal candidate for a Jupiter stone. Albertus Magnus wrote that wearing an amethyst makes the person vigilant and prudent while Hildegard of Bingen used amethyst to heal skin diseases and swellings. It is said that amethyst had calming properties and should be worn in times of nervousness. In Arabic countries, people still put amethyst crystals under their pillows to prevent bad dreams. On a physical level, amethyst helps to get rid of tense headaches and helps with bruises and swellings. It purifies the blood and problems with the lungs and respiratory tract can be eased.

❧

Lapis Lazuli

Lapis Lazuli is technically a sodium aluminium silicate, formed during the metamorphosis of chalk into marble. It consists of a mixture of minerals among which are lazurite, pyrite and calcite. It has a cubic crystal structure and a Mohs hardness of 7. The name 'lapis lazuli' derives from the Latin *lapis*, for 'stone', and the Persian *lazhward*, which can be translated as 'blue'. In ancient Sumer, the lapis lazuli was connected with deities in general indicating its correspondence with Jupiter. It was believed that a person, carrying this stone, could make use of the divine forces, as it contained the power of all of divinity. On the material level, lapis lazuli can help to lower a person's blood pressure, which falls under Jupiter's rulership. It has a relatively high content of sulphur and is therefore thought to help with anaemia. It is also said to regulate the function of the thyroid gland. On an emotional level, lapis lazuli encourages self-awareness, but can also help to face the truth if we are confronted with it. The stone is also used as an antidepressant and in times past was drunk with freshly collected dew. Earlier sources seem to refer to lapis lazuli when mentioning stones with the name of *saphirus*. More will be added in the entry dealing with the sapphire.

❧

Sapphire

Sapphire is the blue variety of corundum composed of aluminium and coloured by iron and titanium. If oriented rutile needles are present in the sapphire, they give rise to a star formation also known as an asterism and are called star sapphires. The sapphire's hardness is 9 on the Mohs scale which is equal to that of ruby. This makes it the second hardest crystal after the diamond. The Greeks attributed the sapphire to the god Apollo and it was often used as an oracle stone, for example at Delphi. Kunz remarks in his book *The Curious Lore of Precious Stones* that William Langley already mentions sapphire as a cure for disease in his work *The Vision of William Concerning Piers the Plowman*, which was written in 1377. Care has to be taken when reading earlier sources because until the 13th century the name *saphirus* also referred to lapis lazuli. From the early 12th century onwards, Christian bishops were encouraged to wear a sapphire ring, symbolising purity. Besides bishops, priests and prelates, the concepts of purity and honour fall under the rulership of Jupiter. John Maplet tells us in his *Greene Forest,* that:

"The sapphir is sky coloured or blew, like to the sky in the most faire weather. It is one of the noblest and royal sorts amongst al gems, and most meet to be worn only upon kings and princes fingers. This for his sovereignty of the Lapidary, is called ye Gem of Gems. It is found most especially in India, although that sometimes, otherwhere. Cardane sayth, that it is next and above the adamant in reputation: first or last in the degree of those gems that be noble and precious: he sayth also, it is good (if it be not otherwise overlaid) to the eyesight, and that nothing in the whole world, doth more recreate or delight the eyes than smaragde & sapphir do. Albertus Magnus saith, that he hath proved it twice, that with the only touching of this precious stone, the party so diseased, hath been rid of the grievous sore the carbuncle. It is marvellously effective against al venom. Wherefore, if thou put a spider into a bor, and upon the mouth of the bor, being shut thou layest the true sapphir and keep the spider but a very short time within the same, the spider being vanquished and overcome by such mean of close virtue dieth suddenly. In old time it was consecrated only to Apollo: for the which they thought their business in wars and affaires at home might be the sooner ended, if through such means they had enriched and honoured him, who by oracle in all things those which were weightiest made only the answer."

The name 'sapphire' stems from the Arabic word *sapphirus,* after the research by Firuzadesch. Some sources claim that the word derived from the Syriac *saphilah.* Other researchers state that, according to the Talmud, the tables of the law were fashioned of sapphire and the word is therefore connected to the Hebrew root *safar,* meaning 'to engrave' as well as 'to shine'. Hildegard of Bingen called the sapphire a stone "symbolising wisdom". Albertus Magnus writes that he had seen a sapphire used as an eyestone, for the removal of foreign bodies from the eye. The stone is used to encourage the physical healing process, particularly in intestinal diseases and helps to lower fevers. It is said to be a useful remedy against heart problems. Generally the sapphire is seen as a stone that can help to find one's hidden potential and can also help to achieve a balanced perspective on life.

Sapphire of a lighter blue can also be used in correspondence with Venus problems and imperial topaz, which is of an orange colour, may be used as a Sun stone. These will be dealt with separately in individual entries.

໒᠕ᕽ

Topaz

John Maplet tells us about the topaz and the imperial topaz:

> "The topaz as Pliny sayth, is a Gem of grassy colour: although that in Germany it is found like to gold. It was first found in Arabia, in a certain land there: whereas the people troglodyte such as live by snake's flesh and other serpents, being compelled through very extreme hunger: and they also being on the water or sea, drive thither by tempest, and so both weary and hungry, digging up the roots of certain herbs, by hap and chance pulled up this. This land afterwards was sought of mariners and merchants, and was ransacked where as they found (having had of them knowledge hereof) their best merchandise. After that, for those people's sake, by whom they had so won and done so well, they would never change the name hereof, but after their proper and peculiar speech called it a topaz. For *topazein* in Greek is as much, as to find by seeking. Pliny sayth, that it hath been found of that bigness and quantity that Philadelphus is said to have framed, and made thereof a statue length of four cubits."

John Maplet is correctly quoting Pliny, but neither of them was aware that the true topaz was unknown to the ancients. What they called 'topaz' was really a chrysolite. Topaz is formed magmatically, has a Mohs hardness of 8 and has an orthorhombic crystal structure. Chromium gives topaz a yellow colour, manganese brownish, and iron blue. Although topaz is generally considered to be a stone corresponding to Jupiter, we are only concerned with the blue variety. (The imperial topaz or gold topaz corresponds to the Sun and is described in the appropriate chapter.) It has been said that topaz can have a beneficial influence when dealing with liver problems, can help to prevent spells of anger and can also reduce a person's level of lust. Throughout history, topaz was considered to bring wisdom and self-realisation to the owner and the Greeks believed that it would "calm anacreontic temperaments" (Anacreon was a Greek poet who was well known for his fondness of love and wine). Even nowadays it is said that topaz is a calming stone and that it can bring peace and joy. On a physical level, topaz can help with blood disorders, loss of appetite and problems with the lungs. Furthermore it is said that topaz can improve one's digestion and increase the body's metabolic rate. Hildegard of Bingen used a blue topaz to cure what she called "dimness of the vision". The stone had to be placed in wine for three days and three nights. Before going to sleep, the patient had to rub his eyes with the topaz so that some of the moisture from the stone touched the eyeballs.

√ √

Zircon (Hyazinth, Jacinth):

Zircon is a silicate of zirconia which crystallises in square prisms, terminating in pyramids. It has a Mohs hardness of 7.5 and can be found in white, blue, green yellow and red. In antiquity, zircon was known as hyazinth or jacinth and we have to carefully examine our sources, making sure which gemstone the individual author refers to. The word 'hyazinth' comes from the Persian *yacut*, a ruby, and the name 'zircon' comes from the Arabic word *zerk*, a gem. A legend tells about Hyacinthus, a mythological figure, who was accidentally slain by Apollo because of the god's jealousy of the youth's beauty. The spilt blood produced the hyazinth flower and it is said that its beauty is also reflected in the hyazinth. Hildegard von Bingen writes about the use of hyazinth, but we cannot be sure if her stone is identical with the stone we know as zircon today. It is often supposed that our modern day sapphire was known to the ancients as hyacinthus and some also believe that the iolite, which has often been mistaken for a sapphire in the past, was called hyacinthus. John Maplet was aware of the apparent similarity between zircon and sapphire, as he writes:

> "The jacinct is blew, and of nigh neighbourhood with the sapphire. This is a marvellous turncoat, for that it doth conform it self to all settings and dispositions

of the air, for being held in the cloudy and dark air, becomes also cloudy and dark: and being in the bright and clear air, becomes also both bright and clear. It is taken to be medicinable, to give vigour and strength to the limbs, to increase the sinews, and to provoke quiet and sound sleep."

In connection with Jupiter, we are only interested in the purple, violet, and blue gems and not the white or green varieties. Since antiquity, zircon has been known to help in cases of madness but it was also used to make the wearer more resistant against any kind of temptation. It has also been said that a person who is wearing hyacinth will be amiable in the eyes of human and god alike. It can support us to become more detached from materialistic thoughts and helps us to focus on higher aims. On the mundane level, zircon can help to overcome loss and enables us to release sadness, pain and fear. Blue zircon particularly has a varied range of healing properties: it has liver stimulating and anti-spasmodic effects, helps asthma sufferers and has a beneficial effect on bronchial, lung and general respiratory problems.

Mercury

Mercury's corresponding metal is mercury or quicksilver and his corresponding colours are yellow, blue and green. Lilly says about Mercury, that:

"... we may not call him either Masculine or Feminine, for he is either the one or the other as joined to any planet; for if in conjunction with a Masculine planet, he becomes Masculine; if with a Feminine, then Feminine, but of his own nature he is cold and dry, and therefore Melancholy; with the good he is good, with the evil planets ill."

Gemini and Virgo are his houses and he is exalted in 15 degrees Virgo. Mercury receives detriment in Sagittarius and Pisces and is in his fall in Pisces. His friends are Jupiter, Venus and Saturn; all other planets are his enemies. He rules the air triplicity, being Gemini, Libra and Aquarius by night. Sometimes also known as 'The Messenger of the Gods', Mercury rules the mind, intellect, logic, and speech. He is also ruler of the nervous system and the vocal chords, tongue, and ears. Depending on the placement of Mercury in the nativity or direction, the nerves of the parts of the body in correspondence with that sign will be affected. Debilitated Mercury in Aries, for example, makes the native prone to head colds or trigeminal problems; Mercury afflicted in Cancer may indicate problems with the throat or tongue. Mercury is essentially debilitated if he is in his detriment, fall or peregrination. He is accidentally debilitated if he is in house 6, 8, or 12; if he is retrograde, slow in motion, occidental, under the sunbeams, combust, in partile conjunction with Cauda Draconis, partile conjunction with Mars, partile opposition with Mars or partile square with Mars, also if he is in conjunction with fixed star Caput Algol. (The complete tables of essential and accidental dignities and debilities should be consulted to find the possible degree of Mercury's debility in any given chart.) If Mercury is found to be essentially or accidentally afflicted in a nativity, or temporarily debilitated through other influences, agate, opal or turquoise may be used as a remedy.

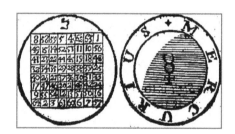

Agate (Achates)

Agate is basically solidified chalcedony that is deposited in layers. It has a Mohs hardness of between 6.5 and 7. The bands, so typical for the agate, are formed through the deposition of different substances between the layers. These can be, for example, rock crystal, amethyst, jasper or onyx. Therefore the appearance and colour of agate can vary widely. Throughout history, many different names have been allocated to agates containing different semi-precious stones. We have already mentioned jaspachates (jasper), smragdachates (emerald), and so forth. John Maplet had this to say about the agate:

"Achates is a kind of gem, but lack in colour, interlined here & there with white veins: and it is called Achates of a certain flout of that name in Sicily, about the which flout this Achates was first found. There is a certain kind hereof seen sometimes in Crete as Diascorides witnessed, having strokes on each side like to blew veins. There is another kind in India be-spotted on every part with spots like blood. That of Crete is said to make a man gracious, and to bring him in favour. That of Indie is good for the eyesight it remedies venom, and being put into the fire is odoriferous."

Although Maplet has his own theory, we also know that Theophrastus, a Greek philosopher, was the first to discover the stone along the river Achates, naming it thus. It is said that agate increases the wearer's ability to speak in public. The stone is harmonising and can stabilise health. It may be of help to combat problems with ears and tongue which might have lead to deafness or disorder of speech. Agate stones were often set into rings which helped the person wearing it to seem more persuasive, eloquent and fluent in expression. In the Middle Ages, agate was used to combat coughs and throat problems. All of these descriptions demonstrate that agate was generally used to help against ailments falling under the rulership of Mercury. It is also said that agate can be of help when suffering from diseases of the eyes, gastritis and stomach ulcers. Three types of agate are of special interest to the astrologer: the yellow, blue and green agate. Yellow agate is particularly used to stimulate the mind and is said to increase creativity. Blue lace agate may be used to achieve a balanced state of mind. Green agate, which is nowadays known as chrysoprase, is especially worn to prevent diseases of the eyes.

❧⚓

Chrysolith (Olivine, Peridot, Topazion)

Chrysolith is formed in deep rock out of alkaline magma, has an orthorhombic crystal structure and a Mohs hardness of 6.5 to 7. Care has to be taken when we read about the properties and the use of the 'chrysolith' in traditional sources. Reason for this is the fact that this name was usually given to either topaz or jacinth. These days it is the olivine with its distinctive transparent green colour which is also known as chrysolith. In the past, the stone was also known as 'topazion', and the Greek historian Strabo wrote "the topazion from the island of Ophiodes near Egypt is a golden yellow (from the Greek *chrysoeidês*), translucent stone, glowing so much, that it cannot be seen during the day". It could only be spotted and collected during the night. To make matters even more complicated, some medieval authors referred to the olivine as 'topaz', which only adds to the confusion. Another name for chrysolith is 'peridot' which may be derived from the Arab word *al-Batra*, simply meaning, 'stone'. Today, the name peridot is mainly used for olivine of gemstone quality sold by jewellers. We know that the ancient Egyptians made use of chrysolith's healing properties at least as far back as 2000 BC. The Romans also knew that this stone could help to increase personal protection against enemies, and to ward off illusions. Today, it is utilised to enhance our ability to communicate and is thought to be able to create and to strengthen friendship. It is also believed that peridot can help to make the wearer more assertive and improve their self-confidence. All of these uses show its connection with the planet Mercury.

Opal

Opal is formed through the solidification of silicic acid gel which occurs through a loss of water and the remaining water surrounds tiny silicon dioxide globules. Due to this internal structure the opal diffracts light and it is this bending of light that gives the gemstone its many different colours. Where the base colour is blueish it is called boulder opal, where it is black we speak of black opals, and where it is white it is called milk opal. Pliny writes in the first century AD that in the opal, one "shall see the living fire of ruby, the glorious purple of the amethyst, the sea-green of the emerald, all glittering together in an incredible mixture of light". Because the colours of the ruby, garnet, emerald, and amethyst can all be seen in the opal, some admirers claimed that the gemstone possessed the therapeutic and prophylactic powers of all these stones. John Maplet writes about the opal in his *Greene Forest*:

"Oppalus (as saith Diascorides) is a stone in colour like to very many, and those clean contrie Gems. For it represents in some part as good a green colour as the Smaragde: in some other part it looks like Purple, and in another part like to a hot coal as the Carbuncle doth."

It is said that the name opal is derived from *pupillus*, the apple of the eye. According to Greek mythology, opals were formed from the tears of Zeus which he shed when he was overjoyed by the victory over the Titans. The Aztecs believed that opals were the earthly manifestations of the waters of paradise and, in India, opals are believed to be the beautiful Goddess of Rainbows who turned into stone to escape the advances of other gods. Pliny knew that the opal, "in consequence of its extraordinary beauty, has been called *paederos* (lovely youth), by many authors; and some who make a distinctive species of it say that it is the same as the stone that is called *sangenon* in India and *taenites* in Egypt". He also tells us that the opal is beneficial for the eyes, but could also strengthen the inner eye and increase psychic abilities. Boulder opals, black opals and milk opals are all used for Mercury problems, as described above. Opals are seen as stones that can enhance creativity and imagination; they may also help to increase the wearer's ability to memorise information. The blue opal is particularly used for the realisation of all forms of wishes; the black opal is used to enhance sexual attractiveness and is capable of the transformation of fear into optimism.

৯৽৶

Turquoise

The turquoise, or Turkish-stone, is a phosphate of alumina, tinted with iron or copper phosphate which are responsible for the blue and green colours of the gemstone. It has a Mohs hardness of 6. Depending on its individual colour, a turquoise can either be used as a Venus or a Mercury stone. Pliny knew that the turquoise's colour spectrum ranged between blue and green. He writes that *callais*, a form of turquoise, "is like sapphirus in colour, only that it is paler and more closely resembling the tint of the water near the seashore in appearance". He also mentions another variety, called *callaina*, which resembles the colour of emeralds. John Maplet writes that:

"The Turches or Turcois, is of the common sort called Eranus. It is in colour air-like or like to the Heavens, and looks clear also as sayth Cardane. It is called a Turches for that it is only found in Turkland or amongst the Turks. This hath such virtue and hidden manner in working, that it supports and sustains, being worn in a ring, a man from falling of his horse, and is said of the above said author to receive the danger of the fall it self, and to break and burst in sunder, rather than the man should fall and miscarry."

The Arabs call the turquoise *fayruz* or *firuzaj*, which means 'lucky stone'. Mounted in a ring or pendant, a necklace, or earrings, the turquoise is said to protect the wearer from poison or poisonous insect bites. The 17th century astrologer John Partridge listed all kinds of poison under the rulership of Venus. If one would wear a turquoise to try and diminish the risk of being poisoned, a green coloured stone should be chosen. In Arabia it is also claimed that the person who wears a turquoise will be warned about the approach of death by the stone changing its colour. Oriental lore has it that the liquid a turquoise has been dipped in or washed with, can be used as a palliative for those who suffer from painful urination (a Venus disease, according to the astrologer William Lilly). Turquoise is used to help with stomach problems and it is said that it can increase the activity of the human brain. We know that stomach problems are connected with Venus and brain activity falls under Mercury's rulership. Turquoise can help to induce calmness while being alert and responsive at the same time. These days, it is used mainly for mental balance, peace of mind and inner calm and in such cases a turquoise of blue colour will turn out to be most helpful.

Mars

Mars' corresponding metal is iron and his corresponding colour is red. He is a masculine, nocturnal planet and his nature is hot and dry. Aries is the day house and Scorpio the night house of Mars. He governs the water triplicity, being Cancer, Scorpio and Pisces. Mars is called 'The Lesser Infortune' because he is considered to be a malefic planet. He is exalted in 28 degrees Capricorn, in his detriment in Libra and Taurus and in his fall in Cancer. His action is acutely violent, unlike Saturn, known as the 'Greater Infortune', whose action is slow and chronic. Mars' only friend is Venus; all other planets are his enemies. The qualities of Mars are hot, dry, barren, antagonistic, caustic, excessive, vicious, reckless, intensive, malicious and disruptive. He is associated with the element of fire and the choleric temperament. Mars rules over the genitals and generative organs, blood and particularly haemoglobin, secretions and the muscles of the bowels. Diseases of Mars are quick burning fevers and inflammations, measles, smallpox, ruptures of blood vessels, wounds where there is loss of blood, like stab wounds from daggers or swords and from war. High blood pressure, kidney or bladder stones and venereal diseases are also typical of Mars when debilitated. Saunders wrote that Mars in the last twelve degrees of Taurus suggests "the stone in the reins and gravel" and Mars in Virgo causes "the stone in the bladder". Mars is essentially debilitated if he is in his detriment, fall or peregrination. He is accidentally debilitated if he is in house 6, 8 or 12; if he is retrograde, slow in motion, occidental, under the sunbeams, combust, in partile conjunction with Cauda Draconis, also if he is in conjunction with fixed star Caput Algol. Fixed stars of Mars' nature are Aldebaran, Antares, Castor, Pollux, Regulus and Sirius. (The complete tables of essential and accidental dignities and debilities should be consulted to find the possible degree of the debility of Mars in any given chart.) If Mars is found to be essentially or accidentally afflicted in a nativity or temporarily debilitated through other influences, carnelian, garnet, haematite, red jasper or magnetite may be used as a remedy. For the healing qualities of green jasper, heliotrope and blue chalcedony, which correspond to Venus, please see the appropriate entries.

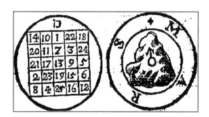

Carnelian (Sard, Red Sardonyx)

Carnelian is a form of chalcedony containing iron, with a trigonal crystal structure and a Mohs hardness of 7. The blue-green variety of chalcedony, called copper chalcedony, is described in its own entry, under Venus stones. John Maplet wrote the following about carnelian:

"The Cornellis is one of those sortes that be somewhat rare also, but not so precious, and is coloured red almost like to the Corall. It being hung about the neck, or worne upon the finger, is said, in all kinds of reasoning and disputation, to appease the party that weareth it, and to keepe him from childish brawlings."

Hildegard of Bingen is thought to have been the first person to distinguish between the red and the brown varieties of the carnelian. The name 'sard' is generally only applied to the red chalcedony. The sardonyx, as its name suggests, is a variety of chalcedony with alternate layers of red and white chalcedony, or onyx. John Maplet knew about the sardonyx, writing:

"Sardonyx, as the Lapidare saith, is red and brown of the Sardye, which is the father to him, Onyx, which we before mentioned, in maner his mother. … This in working maketh a man lowly and shamefast in his doings."

For more about black onyx, see its entry under Saturn stones. The iron content of carnelian immediately reveals that this gemstone is connected to the planet Mars. Its styptic qualities have been known for hundreds of years. Nowadays we know that carnelian can encourage the absorption of vitamins and minerals through the small intestines. It is also known to purify and cleanse a person's blood and to encourage the formation of new blood cells. Some sources also claim that carnelian helps the individual to develop a high level of courage and gives the ability to overcome difficulties.

৯৩৯৩

Garnet (Carbunculus Garamanticus)

Garnet is a group of minerals consisting of a number of different representatives. All of them belong to the cubic crystal system and all of them were formed during the formation of metamorphic rocks. The following are some of the garnets known so far, that include the almandine, whose colours range from violet to red or even black. The name is said to be a corruption of Pliny's *alabandine*, referring to the garnet being cut and polished in Alabanda, a Turkish city. Essonite, which is also known as 'cinnamon stone', has a reddish to yellow tint. Pyrope, which is sometimes called 'fire garnet' due to its fiery dark red colour and is found mainly in Bohemia and Germany. Vermillion garnet of orange red colour, and uvarovite which is emerald green in colour. However, we are concerned mainly with the red varieties of garnet, also known as carbunculus. It has to be noted that not only garnet, but also ruby and balas ruby (rose tinted spinel) were at times called carbuncle. Ruby, which is ruled by the Sun, is described in depth in the chapter dealing with Sun stones. Some authors distinguished between carbunculus garamanticus, which we know as garnet, and carbunculus indicus, also known as ruby. It was believed that these stones would glow in the dark, hence the term *carbunculus*, meaning 'little coal'. John Maplet tells us that:

> "The Carbuncle is a stone very precious, so called for that (like to a fiery coal) it giveth light, but especially in the night season: it so warreth with the pupil or the eyesight, that it shows manifold reflexions. It has as some say fifteen kinds: but those most precious that come nigh the Carbuncles nature: it is found in Libya."

Garnet has always been connected with warriors and heroes dealing with dangerous and difficult tasks to show their commitment and courage and achieving the seemingly impossible. It was also used as a protection stone and it was believed that the carbuncle lost its brilliance, becoming dull, when the wearer was in imminent danger. In Italy, garnets are known as *pietro della vedovanza*, the stone of widowhood. Widows wore necklaces made of garnet beads assuring the wearer eternal love and faithfulness. Some sources claim that the name 'garnet' comes from the Latin *granaticus*, a grain, which may be in reference to the pomegranate (malum garanatum), a fruit with red seeds similar to some garnet crystals. Theophrastus states that the Greek word synonymous with garnet was *anthrax,* signifying a glowing piece of coal. It is said that garnet has calming qualities and can be used against depression and mental unrest, promoting self-confidence and hope. It is also known as the most useful stone in times of a crisis. Potency problems may be reduced and some report a restorative function of the sexual balance. Garnet boosts the immune system and helps with the healing of wounds. Alamandine is particularly beneficial for wound healing and Pyrope stimulates blood circulation and formation of blood. Grossularite, a pinkish garnet, is believed to protect the kidneys and helps to ease the pain of arthritis and rheumatism.

ॐ৺ॐ

Haematite (Ematites or Bloodstone)

Haematite is an iron oxide mineral of metallic grey colour with a Mohs hardness of 6.5. Since the Middle Ages it has also been known as bloodstone and some believe that the reason for this that the water, used in the polishing process, became blood red. Theophrastus described haematite, being of "a dense, solid texture, dry, or, according to its name, seeming as if formed of concrete blood". It should be noted that through the centuries the name 'bloodstone' has also been applied to carnelian, red agate, heliotrope, red jasper, and red marble. John Maplet tells us that:

> "Ematites is a stone somewhat ruddy, somewhat sanguine, found both in Africa, in India and in Arabia: so named for that it resolves & changes often into a bloody colour: and is called of some stench blood, for that it stops his vent or course of flowing."

Zachalius of Babylon writes in his book of gemstones that haematite brings luck to the wearer and makes it possible for him to win any court case or battle. There is one particular kind of tawny coloured haematite which was known to the Greeks as *xanthos*. When pulverised and ingested with wine it stopped blood loss. It is generally believed that haematite has styptic qualities and was used principally to stop blood flowing out of stab wounds caused by iron blades. The red powder of the haematite was also used to clear blood-shot eyes, to cure snake bites and to stop bleeding in the lungs and uterus. It is thought that if a woman wears a ring with a haematite set into it, she will have an easy childbirth. It is also believed that haematite can help with bladder problems because traditionally, the bladder is ruled by Scorpio, one of the signs Mars rules over. In parts of the Sudan, bloodstone is worn as a protection from sunstroke or headache. Modern day research has shown that the presence of haematite increases the absorption of iron in the small intestine and is said to improve the body's oxygen supply.

൪൦ഔ

Jasper (Iaspar, Iaspis):

Jasper is a chalcedony, basically consisting of fine-grained quartz mixed with many foreign materials and has a Mohs hardness of 7. As a result of its different additional materials, Jasper comes in a vast range of colours. The three basic ones are yellow, green and red. We are interested in the red one here, the green variety, called heliotrope, is connected with Venus and is described in the chapter dealing with Venus stones. John Maplet knew that:

> "The Iaspar is a gem very green, like to the Smaragde, but of little more gross colour. Isidor saith that this has 17 several kinds and he calls it the green stone. That of Cyprus, (saith Harmolaus) is more dusky coloured and gross: That of Persia is like to the air, for the which it is called Aerizula: That of Phrygia is purple coloured: There hath been in ancient time seen a Jasper in weight 11 ounces. There is also in the head of the serpent Aspis found a little stone much like to the Jasper of marvellous virtue, which some by cutting away the first letter, have called Aspis. It is thought to have so many ways in working as it has kinds."

It is generally believed that the name 'jasper' comes from the Hebrew *jashpeh*. Jasper is also sometimes called *lapis ophites hadschar elhaijat*. Some ancient authors state, though, that this would be dark vermilion rather than jasper. One of the earliest sources, Diascorides, thinks that *lapis ophites* would be some kind of jasper, but perhaps also an emerald. *Lapis ophites*, or *ophietis* is also known as the 'snake stone'. Powdered jasper was often used as an ingredient in preparations given to women. It was thought to prevent the wearer from being lethargic. The stone was also worn by women with small children because it was thought that the jasper would increase the amount of milk available for breast feeding. Pregnant women wore jasper to prevent having nightmares. Some writers have gone as far as to say that jasper was used as a contraceptive. The egyptologist Wallis Budge writes that the Egyptians associated jasper with the blood of the goddess Isis, and later on in the Middle Ages, the stone was used to stop nose bleeds or to regulate excessive menstruation. Some medieval texts indicate that jasper has the ability to prevent blood from flowing out of wounds or orifices. Sir John Mandeville writes in his *Reis van Jan van Mandeville* that jasper with bright red spots, called *dyaspre,* would, when ground to a powder, curb blood flow. Dyaspre was also believed to heal the bites of snakes. All of which indicates the close correspondence between jasper and Mars and which is also depicted on the famous Abrasax stones. These are pieces of jasper, which bear engraved depictions of Mars, holding a shield in his left and a weapon in his right hand. Quite often snakes or vipers replace his feet. Gnostics used Abrasax stones as amulets.

৵৽৻

Magnetite (Lodestone)

Magnetite is a magnetic iron ore of iron-black colour and has a metallic lustre. Polished and cut into facets, it resembles the brightness of polished steel. During the Middle Ages, magnetite was often called 'mariner's stone', referring to the compass needle. John Maplet already knew that:

> "The Lodestone comes from India, and is almost iron colour like. It is found most rife amongst the Trogloditas people, in the furthest part of Africa, beyond Ethiopia, who are said to dwell in caves, and to eat serpent's flesh. It draws iron to it, even as one lover cutes and desires an other. The common people therefore having sometime seen this so done by secret and unknown working, have judged and reputed ye iron lively. There is another kind of Lodestone in Thessalie, that is of contrary set and disposition, which will have none of iron, nor will meddle with it. But for the other that is reckoned principal and best, which in colour is blue. Saint Augustine saith, that if any man put under any vessel either golden or brass, or hold under these any piece of iron, and lay above the vessels or upon them this Lodestone, that even through the very motion or moving of the stone underneath, the Iron shall move up and meet with it as nigh as the vessel will suffer at the very top."

Pliny, quoting Nicander, states that the lodestone got its name from a shepherd who first discovered it in Mount Ida. It is said that the magnetite attracted the nails in the soles of his shoes and the ferule of his staff when he walked over the bed. Others claim that its name derives from the ancient city of Magnesia in Thessaly where it was once mined. Magnetite was first mentioned in Plato's *Timaeus* in which he gave it the name 'stone of Herakles', because it was mined in Heraklea, but Homer, Epicure, Pythagoras and Aristotle mention the lodestone as well. It is said to help dispel melancholy, to have calming properties and to induce a deep, dreamless sleep. Like the haematite it has styptic qualities. Magnetite can relieve pains in hands and feet and is also useful against arthritis, swellings in general and liver problems. Wearing lodestone often supports women in labour. Wallis Budge wrote that a Dr. Campbell-Thompson had shown that the Assyrians called the magnetite *shadanu sabitu*, which translates to 'the haematite which grabs or attracts'. He continues that before sexual intercourse the man mixed the magnetite with oil and rubbed himself with the mixture. The woman rubbed herself with *parzilli*, which is iron powder, to increase her power of attraction for the man. It was also believed that drinking water wherein a piece of magnetite had been steeped could cure a person from epilepsy. This can be explained if we consider that, according to traditional sources, Aries has rulership over epilepsy. Aries is, of course, the day house of Mars, under whose rulership magnetite falls.

Venus

Venus' corresponding metal is copper and her corresponding colour is green. Taurus and Libra are the houses of Venus. She is exalted in 27 degrees Pisces, in her detriment in Aries and Scorpio. She is in her fall in 27 degrees Virgo. Venus governs the earth triplicity by day, being Taurus, Virgo and Capricorn. She is a feminine, nocturnal, passive, negative, benign planet and her nature is temperately cold and moist, although in some cases she is considered to be warm. She is called 'The Lesser Fortune' and her action is slow. All planets, except Saturn are friends of Venus. The qualities of Venus are negative, nutritive, relaxing and nourishing. She is associated with the elements of air and water and the sanguine and phlegmatic temperament. She rules over the generative system and the genitals, womb, bladder and breasts and is particularly identified with the ovaries. Illnesses ruled by Venus are those arising from excesses connected with desire, love and sex, as well as those arising from weakness or poisoning. Further illnesses are those of the kidneys, back and belly, smallpox, and measles. When afflicted, Venus tends to weaken the generative system. Saunders knew that Venus in Scorpio showed "stopping of the urine, pains of the reins and kidneys, and cramps in women". Venus in Sagittarius causes "diseases in the privy parts, in the matrix and vulva, as burning with women." Venus is essentially debilitated if she is in her detriment, fall or peregrination. She is accidentally debilitated when located in house 6, 8 or 12; if she is retrograde, slow in motion, occidental, under the sunbeams, combust, in partile conjunction with Cauda Draconis, partile conjunction with Mars, partile opposition with Mars or partile square with Mars, also if she is in conjunction with fixed star Caput Algol. (The complete tables of essential and accidental dignities and debilities should be consulted to find the possible degree of the debility of Venus in any given chart.) If Venus is found to be essentially or accidentally afflicted in a nativity, or temporarily debilitated through other influences, aquamarine, beryl, copper chalcedony, heliotrope or emerald may be used as a remedy.

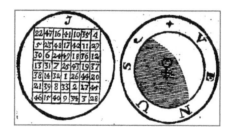

Aquamarine

The aquamarine is a member of the beryl family. Other well-known members of the beryl family are the emerald and the heliodor; the emerald will be described in detail in its own entry. Beryl is colourless when in its pure form, it is the variety of various impurities that give beryls their distinctive colours. All beryls have a Mohs hardness of 7.5. The name 'aquamarine' comes from the Latin, *aqua marina*, which translates as 'water of the sea'. Pliny called the aquamarine *thalassus angites*. John Maplet writes in his *Greene Forest* that:

"Berill is a stone rare, but not so precious, for it alone grows in India: it is found green like to the Smaradge. It is first found also raw and rude without either good look or pleasant shelve, but afterwards it is better polished of them of India, and they use to polish it in manner and form of angle or corner, to the intent that through ye dullness of his own colour, this manner might show some glittering the light having his stay in every each corner: Some say, they fashion it at the first seven cornered: and otherwise they say it shimmers not. There is also another kind of Berill, which of the Greek word is called Golden Berill, as says Diascorides, whose interchanged green colour resembles almost the wan and yellow colour of gold. They say that this being borne about a man, and being put now and then to his eyes, keeps a man out of peril of his enemies."

During the Middle Ages it was believed that all beryls were made out of water that had been congealed for seven years. It is said that aquamarine makes the person wearing the stone lucky and wealthy but chaste and humble at the same time. It also strengthens marital bonds. Beryl helps to reduce nervousness and stress and raises self-confidence. It has a detoxifying effect and can stimulate the liver. Aquamarine was also used as a remedy to stop vomiting. The astrologer William Lilly states in his *Christian Astrology* that "the desire to vomit" would fall under the rulership of Venus. If a person was afflicted by throat problems, the remedy against this was thought to be the repeated ingestion of aquamarine water. The throat falls under the rulership of Taurus and Venus which explains this connection. Beryl is also used in cases of long- and short-sightedness. We also know that the ancient Greeks used the refracting properties of beryl to construct the first known eyeglasses. The word 'Brille', which is the German word for spectacles, reminds us of that fact. Hildegard of Bingen thought that aquamarine would bring a bringer of peace. She also prescribed spring water that had a "moderate amount of beryl grated into" as a remedy against poisoning. After five days of drinking beryl water, the poison would either "foam out through nausea, or pass through [the patient's] posterior".

ॐ

Copper Chalcedony

Chalcedony is a mixture of silica in the states of quartz and opal. In it purest form it is quite colourless, but when mixed with small quantities of other substances, chalcedony forms a variety of brilliantly coloured gemstones. John Maplet wrote the following about chalcedony:

> "Calcedon, is a kind of stone, pale wand wan, of dull colour, almost a meane between the Berill and the Jacinth. It has three only kinds: whereof every one of them is almost impossible to be graven in. It being well chafed and warmed, it will draw to it, a straw or a rush. It is as they say, a Lawyers and Orators friend, and others who plead causes."

Descriptions of onyx, agate, carnelian, jasper and heliotrope, which are chalcedonies, mixed with metals or other minerals, can be found throughout this book. Here we are interested in the blue green variety also known as the 'copper chalcedony' due to its inclusions of copper. During the gemstone's formation, the copper is initially dissolved by the silicic acid and later preserved in its metallic form. The name 'chalcedony' comes from the Latin *chalcedonius*, and is probably derived from Chalcedon, a town in Asia Minor. Chalcedony has a trigonal crystal structure and a Mohs hardness of 7. Since time immemorial, copper chalcedony has been valued for its calming effect. A person wearing this gemstone will most certainly experience its relaxing properties. During the Renaissance, copper chalcedony was prescribed to cure phantasms and to prevent hallucinations. It was also believed that a woman, who owned a chalcedony when she got married, would always be loved by her husband. Nowadays we know that copper chalcedony encourages the metabolism of copper in the body. This can have a detoxifying effect. It is also said that this gemstone can help to prevent inflammations of the female sexual organs.

❧

Emerald (Smaragde)

Emerald is a beryllium-aluminium silicate of deep green colour. The beryllium itself is colourless and the radiant colour is due to chromium compounds. Emerald has a Mohs hardness of between 7 and 8. According to Pliny, the emerald takes third rank in esteem after the diamond followed by pearls in second place. He thinks that "there is no stone, the colour of which is more delightful to the eye, there being no green in existence of a more intense colour than this". John Maplet says about the stone that:

> "The Smaragde hath his name of his excellent and fresh green colour. For every thing that is grassy green, is properly called in Greek smaron. It passes both the leaf and bough of any tree or plant in this his colour, and in this point alone triumphs, neither is the Sun by his Sunbeams, any let or hinderance to this his show. There is no greater refection to the eyes than the sight of this. It being polished and dressed, shows a man his lively image, whereupon the valiant Caesar had no greater delight, than in looking on this, to see his warriors fight, and to behold in the Smaragde which of them went best to work, and was most active. Isidore says, that there be twelve kinds hereof, but the most noble is found in Scithia, the next in Bactria. This stone says Cardane, serves to divination, and to tell of a certainty, things to come, or otherwise. For that that shall come to pass, it will never let it sink or slip out of mind, and that shall not, it easily suffers the mind to forget."

In the Middle Ages, emerald was used as an antidote for poisoning. Emerald was also often used to cure diseases of the eyes and it has been said that it was used to cure epilepsy and the 'semitertian' fever. This is a malarial fever in which two paroxysms occur on one day and one on the next day. Emerald also has a detoxifying effect and helps against rheumatism, it also strengthens the immune system and can be used to speed recovery after an infection. Theophrastus knew that the use of emerald to rest and relieve the eye was mentioned as early as the third century BC. An Arab author went as far as to write down an account wherein he states that, after eating a poisonous herb, he placed an emerald in his mouth and one on his stomach and was entirely cured soon after. Hildegard of Bingen used the emerald to "heal all weaknesses and illnesses of mankind". Certain Hindu physicians considered the emerald to be a good laxative, thought it to cure the dysentery and diminished the secretion of bile. Emerald is also said to help with gastric problems. In Germany it was said that an emerald, given as a present to a bride or a lover, would turn brown like dying autumn leaves the moment she was unfaithful.

❧

Heliotrope (Elutropia)

Heliotrope is a green chalcedony and has a Mohs hardness of 6.5 to 7. It is interspersed with small patches of opaque bright red jasper. For this reason it is also often called blood jasper. For more information about red jasper, see the appropriate entry under Mars stones. If no spots of red jasper are present, the green chalcedony is called jaspis. John Maplet knew that:

> "Elutropia is a gem, in colour green, or grassy, in part coloured and bespotted with Purple specs & blood coloured vains. This is a marvellous juggler, for it will cause things object to be presented to our eyes as it lifts. It being put into a basin of water changes to a mans eyesight the Sun his beams, and giveth them a contrary colour. Being also moved and beaten in the air, makes to appear a bloody Sun, and darkens the air in manner of an eclipse: and therefore it is called Eloutropia as you would say, the Sunne his enemy. There is of this name also a certain herb which enchanters & witches have oftentimes used, and do use, as also that above said, whereby they have mocked and deluded many, which by means and working and enchantment, have so dazzled the beholders eyes, that they have gone by them invisibly."

Maplet refers to the plant *Heliotropium sp.* of the borage family. It is said that the name 'heliotrope' comes from the Greek, whereby *Helios* means 'Sun' and *tropein* means 'to turn'. The stone is said to turn the rays of the setting Sun into a blood red colour and the plant, also known as 'turnsole', turns its head towards the Sun. In medieval times it was believed that adepts of magic could mix a paste of the ground stone and the plant of the same name rendering the bearer invisible. Heliotrope is said to boost the immune system and is used in cases of infections, it detoxifies and helps against inflammation and poisoning and it is also often used to prevent discord and to disperse anger. Pliny wrote about green chalcedony: "Jaspis is green and often transparent. That of India is like smaragdus in colour". In ancient China, it was believed that jaspis could help to unravel the mysteries of life. It was also used to concentrate on and discover the invisible world, thus making it visible to the eyes of the person wearing the stone. Even today, Taoists are convinced that jaspis strengthens the body and prolongs physical life. Green jasper is also said to help against poisoning. There are records in existence showing that the Byzantine emperor Manuel presented the monks on Athos with a cup made of green jasper which had strong healing properties and was said to neutralise many poisons.

Sun

The Sun's corresponding metal is gold and his corresponding colour is orange. He is a masculine, diurnal planet and his nature is hot and dry, although more temperate than Mars. Leo is the house of the Sun; he is exalted in 19 degrees Aries and in his fall in 19 degrees Libra. The Sun governs the fiery triplicity by day comprising Aries, Leo and Sagittarius. All planets are friends of the Sun, except Saturn, who is his enemy. The qualities of the Sun are expansive, positive, active, and constructive. The Sun rules over the heart, brain and the right eye in men and the left eye in women. Illnesses ruled by the Sun are most importantly those of the heart, brain or eyes. Fevers and inflammations caused by the Sun are rather slow and severe compared to those related to Mars, which tend to be quick and destructive. According to Saunders, the Sun in Aries indicates "yellowness in the eyes" and other eye problems. Problems with the heart are experienced when the Sun is located between 7 and 24 degrees Leo. Strong fevers are particularly experienced if the Sun is located in the first 6 degrees of Virgo or between 7 and 24 degrees Scorpio. Pestilential fevers and pains of the heart are to be expected if the Sun is in the last 18 degrees of Sagittarius. The Sun is essentially debilitated if he is in his detriment, fall or peregrination. He also is accidentally debilitated if he is in house 6, 8, or 12, in partile conjunction with Cauda Draconis, partile conjunction with Mars, partile opposition with Mars or partile square with Mars, also if he is in conjunction with the fixed star Caput Algol. The complete tables of essential and accidental dignities and debilities should be consulted to find the possible degree of the debility of the Sun in any given chart.

If the Sun is found to be essentially or accidentally afflicted in a nativity or temporarily debilitated through other influences, amber, coral, imperial topaz (gold topaz) or ruby may be used as a remedy. For more information about the purple variety of topaz, see the entry under Jupiter.

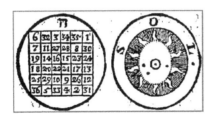

Amber

Amber is a fossilised tree resin with a Mohs hardness of 2.5. It has an amorphous structure and its colour ranges from yellow to golden-orange, although green, red, black and even blue pieces of amber have been found. Amber may have been the first healing stone in the history of humanity, research has shown that pieces of amber have been used as amulets or as healing stones for at least 7000 years. It is warm to the touch and can be electrically charged. Nearly all authors of traditional astrology agree that the Sun has rulership over amber. The Greek name for amber was *elektron*, which translates as 'formed by the Sun'. It was connected to the Sun god Helios, and a Greek myth tells us that, after Helios' son Phaethon was killed by lightning, his sisters were transformed into mourning poplars. The tears they shed each year were said to be pieces of amber. Our modern words 'electricity' and 'electron' are derived from the original Greek word, hinting at the negative electrical charge that can be created in the amber through friction. It has been known for a very long time that amber is a product of pine trees, though, according to Pliny, the Athenian Demostratus called amber *lyncurion*. Demostratus thought that the stone consisted of lynx's urine. From a medical point of view, amber can help against metabolically based skin complaints and encourages the healing of wounds. In times past, amber has been associated with a large number of healing qualities; it was said that a piece of amber could prevent toothache, help to reduce the pains of rheumatism, cure headaches, jaundice and many other ailments. Powdered amber was often mixed with honey and rose oil and was given to patients suffering from bad eyesight or earache. Diluted in water and taken internally, powdered amber was said to relieve stomach pains and to help kidneys, liver, and intestines to perform their functions more effectively and regularly. It was also believed that when suffering from a high fever, holding a piece of amber could reduce one's temperature. Pliny tells us as well that he had seen many farmers' wives wearing strings of amber beads. Apparently this was not only due to the beauty of the amber, but also as a cure for tonsillitis. In times past, amber was also worn as a protection against witches and was used to prevent bad luck. Today it is said that it can dissolve oppositions and encourage creativity; furthermore it brings good luck to the person wearing it and helps in motivating and boosting self-confidence. It is also said to soothe the wearer's nerves. Until the 19th century, German stable owners, convinced that it would protect their horses from supernatural evil and witchery, used to burn a little piece of amber in their stables after the horses were locked up for the night. To unfold its healing properties, amber should be worn in large quantities and over a long period of time. It should also be exposed to the Sun whenever possible.

Coral

Coral, or red coral, is the common name of *Corallium rubrum*, a species of marine coral. Its skeletal remains have been used for amulets and in jewellery making for thousands of years and coral jewellery has been found in prehistoric European burials. Coral has a trigonal crystal structure and a Mohs hardness of 3.5. John Maplet wrote about it in his *Greene Forest*:

> "The Corall growth in the red Sea, and so long as it is and has his being in waters, it is a kind of Wood, but by and by after that it is taken forth of the water and cometh into the air (and his reach) it hardeneth, and becommeth a stone. His boughs under the water are espied white and tender: and being by chance through holdefast Nets in part or parcel brought to land, change also their colour and become red, and for their feeling, are also hard stones. Isidore in his 16th book, *The Mages*, reports that it resisteth Lightnings. Therefore even as much worth and of estimation as is the precious Margaret, that cometh from Indie, so much worth and in estimation, like wise is the Coral by them of Indie. Hereof are said to be two only kinds, the one red and the other white: this last is never found in bigness and in length more than half a foot: that other often bigger and longer. They say it is of power to rid us from all divelish dreams and peevish fantasies."

For a long time, coral, which is also called 'gorgonios', has been classed as being part of the order of Gorgonaceae. Nowadays the name 'Gorgonacea' is no longer considered valid and 'Alcyonacea' is now the accepted name for the order. A connection remains, though, as the name that was given to coral stems from the legend of the Gorgon. It was believed that coral was born from the drops of blood dripping from Medusa's severed head into the sea while Perseus was carrying it. Pliny tells us that, in Roman times, coral was hung around the necks of infants because they were thought to be a protection against danger. Up to the present day, coral is worn by people of Naples as a protection against the malicious effects of *maloccio*, the evil eye. Coral also helps to deal with fear as well as with spells of panic. It is also believed that depression, and nervous conditions are reduced when coral is worn. A piece of coral placed under the pillow during night-time is said to induce peaceful sleep and also to ward off nightmares.

ক্ষৎ

Imperial Topaz (Gold Topaz)

For general information about topaz see the entry in the chapter dealing with Jupiter stones. The imperial or gold topaz counteracts bad moods and calms irritability, particularly when caused by insomnia. Gold topaz can also stimulate a person's metabolism and digestion. According to ancient traditions, this gemstone can staunch the flow of blood and promote relaxation by easing tension. It is also believed that topaz can heighten the level of self-realisation and improve one's self-confidence. Gold topaz is also used to regulate one's generosity and view of reality which underlines its correspondence with the Sun and the sign of Leo.

ক্ষৎ

Ruby (Carbuncle)

Ruby is magmatically formed as a liquid in aluminium rich rocks and belongs to the corundum family. It has a Mohs hardness of 9, making it one of the hardest stones, only surpassed by the diamond. The ruby's red colour is caused by the presence of chromium and may vary from a light rose tint to the deepest red. Rubies, together with diamonds, are considered to be the most precious of all gems. People who could afford them used rubies in amulets as protection from all kinds of witchery, plague, pestilence and famine. The ruby was also often called carbuncle, or *carbunculus indicus*, because of its resemblance to a red-hot coal. The female variety of *carbunculus indicus* was said to be the spinel, while the male variety was the ruby. Other stones were called carbuncle, too, like the garnet, *carbunculus garamanticus*. (For an in depth description of the garnet, see its entry under Mars stones.) It is said that in India the ruby has fifteen different names; one of them is 'King of the Sun'. The Greek philosopher Aristotle calls the ruby *galib al naun*, the bringer of sleep. John Maplet writes in his *Greene Forest* that:

> "The Rubie is a stone which of some is supposed to be found in the crab's head, most commonly red, yet not withstanding sometimes found in yellow colour. It avails against the biting of the scorpion and weasel, if it be applied thereto plaister like."

To find out if a ruby was genuine, the stone was dropped into boiling water and if the water stopped boiling immediately, the owner knew that his ruby was real. Representing life force and inner fire, the ruby has always been seen as a stone of the Sun amongst European and Indian cultures. Hildegard of Bingen was of the opinion that the carbuncle would develop during the time of a lunar eclipse; she thought them to contain the splendour of the Sun's heat. Hildegard also tells us that a ruby could make hallucinations disappear, making it impossible for the airy spirits to bring their phantasms to completion. In medieval times, the water a ruby had been placed in overnight was used to improve the function of the stomach and increase the appetite. Nowadays, it is thought that the ruby helps to overcome lack of energy, restores general health, is rejuvenating and stimulates sexual activity. It also helps to overcome infectious diseases, has blood-cleansing properties and improves blood circulation. It is also said that the ruby has a balancing effect on hyperactivity.

Spinel

Spinel occurs in granite and metamorphic rocks and is often found in conjunction with corundum just like the ruby and the garnet. It has a cubic crystal structure and a Mohs hardness of 8. Spinel comes in various colours and one of the ways to differentiate it from other, seemingly similar stones is that spinel possesses no electrical properties when heated. The name 'spinel' is said to come from the Greek word *spinther* meaning 'to sparkle'. In the past, spinel was also known as balagius, balas ruby, alamandine, or rubicelle. It was believed to be the female variety of carbunculus indicus, differentiating it from the male variety, which was the ruby. To find out if a stone was male or female, one had to compare the appearance of the stones. Had a stone a bright colour with a rich tint, it was considered to be male and was therefore a ruby. If it was a darker stone with less brilliancy, it was considered to be female. Some sources claim that spinels with the colour of red roses were the preferred stones of Lucrecia Borgia. Many famous spinels passed under the name of ruby, possibly the most famous being the one which was given to Edward, Prince of Wales, also known as the Black Prince. Another name for the balas ruby was *lychnis*, as mentioned by Pliny who thought that the name derived from its lustre, which is heightened by the light of a lamp. Worn around the neck, lychnis protects from sorrow and tiredness. Spinel is said to have antidepressant properties and makes its wearer joyful and gracious. It also brings peace and harmony to the person wearing it and their surroundings.

Moon

The Moon's corresponding metal is silver and her corresponding colour is white. The house of the Moon is Cancer. She is exalted in 3 degrees Taurus, in her detriment in Capricorn. She is in her fall in 3 degrees Scorpio. The Moon governs the earth triplicity by night, this being Taurus, Virgo and Capricorn. She is a feminine, nocturnal planet and her nature is cold, moist and phlegmatic. Her enemies are Saturn and Venus. The qualities of the Moon are negative, passive and fruitful. The Moon rules over the stomach, bowels, the left eye in men and the right eye in women. Illnesses ruled by the Moon are menstrual problems, rheumatism, problems of the bladder and the liver, and complaints of the bowels. Due to the changes of the Moon's phases, the time of Full and New Moon have a strong effect on epileptics and people with nervous predispositions. The Full Moon particularly can lead to sensitive people experiencing spells of restlessness and insomnia.

When afflicted, the Moon tends to have a negative effect on the health of women. Saunders knew that the Moon in Aquarius was particularly detrimental for women, indicating the likelihood of "pains and swellings in the bladder and privy parts" and "stopping the urine and whites in women." If the Moon is debilitated in the birth chart or the native has Cancer rising, a weak constitution or a life of ill health tends to be the result. The Moon is essentially debilitated if she is in her detriment, fall or peregrination. She also is accidentally debilitated if she is in house 6, 8 or 12; if she is slow in motion, occidental, under the sunbeams, combust, partile conjunction with Mars, partile opposition with Mars or partile square with Mars, also if he is in conjunction with the fixed star Caput Algol. (The complete tables of essential and accidental dignities and debilities should be consulted to find the possible degree of the debility of the Moon in any given chart.) If the Moon is found to be essentially or accidentally afflicted in a nativity or temporarily debilitated through other influences, moonstone, pearls or rock crystal may be used as a remedy.

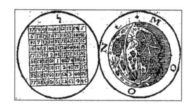

Moonstone

A. Feldspar

What is generally considered to be moonstone now is actually what is known as a water-opal, or potassium feldspar or orthoclase, with a Mohs hardness of 6. It has an innate laminate structure bending the light that gives the polished stone a blueish-white shimmer, which is the reason that this stone has traditionally been assigned to the Moon. Moonstone has a reflecting and calming effect and is predominantly associated with fertility, intuition and emotion. For many hundreds of years it has been used to weave spells of love. It is said that moonstone increases mediumistic abilities and enables the person wearing it to experience lucid dreams and this stone may be used for experiments of clairvoyance particularly at the Full Moon. Moonstone can be helpful in unblocking the lymphatic system and is often used to cure stomach problems. It is also connected with the pineal gland and may help with menstrual problems and during the menopause.

ॐॐ

B. Selenite

In ancient times, people were actually referring to selenite when referring to moonstone. Selenite, also known as desert rose or satin spar, is a variety of gypsum with a Mohs hardness of 2. There is no connection between the feldspar variety and selenite, but it is likely that the silvery shine of the stone may have reminded the ancient Greeks of the Moon goddess Selene. Aristotle knows about selenite, which he calls *bahtah*, that it is a white stone to be found at the end of the most remote darkness, never reached by the Sun's rays and is where one could find *okeanos*, the world-sea. In 1643, Athanasius Kircher wrote that he knew about a selenite with a large white spot on its surface and, during the waxing and waning phases of the Moon, the spot would change accordingly. It is likely that Kircher had read what Pliny had to say about *adaluria*, a particular variety of selenite:

"... white, and transparent, with a reflected colour like that of honey. It has a figure within it like that of the Moon and reflects the face of that luminary, if what we are told is true, according to its phases."

It is also said that Pope Leo X was in possession of a similar moonstone, whose blueish colour changed to white according to the different quarters of the Moon. Marbod said that selenite was "a holy stone" because it cleanses and purifies the emotions and feelings of all humans, but particularly those born with Cancer rising. The ancients believed that selenite assisted the growth of plants in gardens and was also beneficial for fruit trees in orchards. Moonstone is also believed to protect the mind from wandering and can help against epilepsy and insanity. It is also said that selenite attracts positive energies while repelling negative ones. Selenite is a stone of motherhood, associated with fertility and pregnancy. When set into a ring, it grants the person wearing it divine inspiration.

ॐ◌

Pearl (Margaret)

Although regarded as gemstones in the past, pearls are layers of aragonite created around an irritant, like a piece of grit, by shellfish. They have a Mohs hardness of 3. John Maplet, who calls the pearl 'margaret', says:

> "The Margaret of all gems, those which be in their kinds white, is esteemed the chiefest: as Isidore consents, with others herein. Which kind he will also have thus named, for that is found growing in the meat of certain shell fishes, and those of the sea, as in the sea snail, and in the greatest oyster, and such like as have their shell. It is engendered of a certain heavenly dew, which in a certain time of the year, both the sea snail and the cockle doe take and drink up. Of the which kind of stone certain are called onions, for that by one and one, they be found, and never above one: there be some of these also seen sometimes yellow, but the other are the very best."

The name 'margaret' or 'margarita' is said to be the Greek form of the Persian *merwerid*, or the Sanskrit *maracata*. We have seen that Maplet knew about the Christian legend that pearls were created from heavenly dew, but pearls were also often thought to be the tears of goddesses, symbolising innocence and purity. Generally speaking, pearls represent female energy in its purest form and it is claimed that the regular ingestion of pearl-water will harmonise and stabilise the production of hormones. It is said that pearls have a calming and balancing effect. They increase the qualities corresponding to the water element and are sometimes said to tune the person wearing them into the ebb and flow of life. An old German legend states that pearls set in gold represent tears of joy, but set in silver, they symbolise sadness and tears of pain. Furthermore pearls are used to help with stomach problems, skin conditions and allergies. Aristotle thought that pearls would purify the blood of black bile and would also help those suffering from frights and worries.

Hildegard of Bingen writes that pearls should be placed in water and after a while they would attract all the slime from the water, leaving a layer of purified water on the top of the vessel. Those who suffer from a fever should drink from the purified layer of the water to find healing. Hildegard also advises that pearls, heated in the Sun and then placed around the temples, would cure ailments of the head. Mother of pearl, or nacre, which also consists of aragonite, is produced by some molluscs as the top layer of their inner shell. Hildegard of Bingen warns us that it does not have any medicinal use. She claims that nacre, worn on the naked skin, is harmful because the poison in the mother of pearl would be drawn into the body of the wearer making them very ill indeed.

കൗ

Quartz

A. Rock Crystal (Crystal Quartz)

Rock crystal is pure, clear crystal quartz with a Mohs hardness of 7. The name 'quartz' is a derivative of the Greek *crustallos*, meaning ice. John Maplet knew about this, writing:

> "The Cristall is one of those stones that shines in every part, and is varying in colour. Isidore saith, that it is nothing else then a congealed ice by continuance frozen whole years. It grows in Asia and Cyprus, and especially upon the Alps and high mountains of the North Pole. It engenders not so much of the waters coldness, as of the earthiness mixed withal. His property is to abide nothing in quality contrary to itself: therefore it is delighted only with cold."

Crystal quartz is probably the best known, most versatile and most used healing stone of all time. The Greeks used it to drive out evil spirits and diseases and as a burning glass in surgical operations. Powdered quartz was often mixed with honey and given to increase the amount of milk in mothers of small children. It is said that several Scottish clans possessed crystal balls regarded as stones of victory. Hildegard of Bingen believed that rock crystal was born from certain cold, nearly black waters, the cold would congeal these into a lump in some places where the air touched it, then the heat of the Sun touched the mass, transforming it into solid rock crystal. She recommended that people with blurred sight should heat a crystal in the Sun and then place it over the eyes which would improve the eyesight. She also recommended rock crystal as an aid against heart- or stomach-ache. Here the patient should first heat the crystal in the Sun and then pour water over it, after a little while, the crystal should be removed from the water, which should then be drunk frequently for good results. A piece of rock crystal put onto the cheek is said to drive away toothache. Rock crystal has a great ability to stabilise, harmonise and balance our energies as well as our emotions and has great cleansing and enhancing potential. It can revitalise parts of the body that are numb or paralysed. It has a particularly positive effect on the nerves and can reduce fever.

⇛⇝

B. Iris

Iris, a gemstone often mentioned in old texts, is a derivative of rock quartz. It seems to be either hyaline quartz that is internally iridised, or the prismatic crystal of limpid quartz which decomposes the rays of the Sun. This is also where its name comes from, as it projects the colours of the rainbow onto a white surface when struck by a ray of sunlight. John Maplet knew about iris and he had the following to say about it:

> "Iris is a kind of stone mathematically wrought, as being dug up in form fire cornered, which at the first was found nigh the Red Sea: but is now found in many places, as in Germany, in Ireland, and in the North parts and quarters, and is of colour as clear as the Cristall. It is called Iris for likelihood to the rainbow, which being touched & stricken of the Sun his beams, under any covert doth represent and show both the figure and colours of the rainbow upon the wall next to it, and that oppositely, as Diascorides saith, it hath the same force and working that the beryl hath, but is not in quantity so great."

In recent years, iris has been marketed under the name 'rainbow quartz' or 'anandalite', which is thought to mean 'eternal bliss' in Sanskrit.

⇛⇝

PART THREE –

WORKING WITH GEMSTONES

It is clear that every higher body, in virtue of the light which proceeds from it, is the form and perfection of the body that comes after it. The form and perfection of all bodies is light, but in the higher bodies it is more spiritual and simple, whereas in the lower bodies it is more corporeal and multiplied.

(Robert Grosseteste)

In the first part of this book, we established that the four elements represent the different combinations of the four qualities. We also saw that on the next level, which is the zodiac, the four elements are expressed in three different modes. In astrological terminology, these modes are called 'moveable', 'fixed' and 'mutable'. Other systems may recognise them as sattwa, rajas and tamas, or sal, mercury, and sulphur. This led us to the realisation that the twelve signs of the zodiac, together with their mundane counterparts, the mundane houses, are the representation of all of creation. We have also shown how the numbers 1, 2, 3, and 4 are symbols of the creation of the world, resulting in the wheel of the zodiac (3 x 4). Moving one step further into the world of manifestation, we find that the number 5 is the number of the planets used in the tradition which excludes the lights (Sun and Moon). Together with the Sun and the Moon, the number of the planets increases to 7 (3 + 4) as John Dee shows in his depiction of the Monas Hieroglyphica.

In summary, it can be stated that all is essentially one, evidence of which has been given throughout this book. Through the process of creation, this oneness splits into separate parts, comparable to white light splitting into the seven colours of the rainbow when projected through a prism. Expanding this analogy, planets can be compared to single colours representing essentially pure ideas. Other parts created by this split are also in correspondence with each planet's individual essence. Here we find gems, metals, plants, and so forth. Known as the *great chain of being*, this concept was first formulated by Plato, Aristotle and Proclus, becoming fully developed during the Neo-Platonism of the Middle Ages. The great chain of being begins at the divine, and, progressing ever downwards, ends in the manifest world. The higher the links are positioned in this chain, the purer their essence will be. Looking at our astrological planets, we can see that the whole of the essence is split into seven parts. In other words, everything we can possibly think of can be attributed to one of those seven planets. If we take Venus as an example, we can say that she represents the essence of love and beauty in its purest form. We also know that in a human being this Venusian essence is rarely found in its purest form, the level of its refined presence differing from person to person. We also know that, astrologically speaking, every single individual consists of a mixture of the essences of all the seven planets. To establish how much of each planet's essence is present in a person, we have to erect their birth chart to determine the planets' locations at the time of birth. According to their placement, the planets can be delineated/assessed/judged as essentially dignified or debilitated. In other words, the level of dignity or debility symbolises the quantity of each planet's pure essence that has been allotted to this particular person in this life. To standardise these levels, astrologers devised a weighting system, determining the essential strength or weakness of each planet in a given position. A tabulated summary of these is reproduced in part one of this book. To sum it all up, we can say that a debilitated planet in one's birth chart represents a lack of this particular planet's pure essence or a corrupt form of it. In the case of Venus, our earlier example, we can see that a person with a debilitated Venus will experience problems with desire, love, and sex. Depending on the house placement of Venus in the birth chart, there may also be problems with kidneys, bladder or genitals. To counteract this particular debility, it is advisable to wear aquamarine, emerald, or heliotrope. The explanation for this action is thus. If we look at the Neo-Platonic chain of being, once again, we will find that the essence of a gemstone, metal or plant, corresponding to Venus is essentially purer than the person's debilitated Venus. By surrounding the afflicted person with the appropriate gemstones, plants and the corresponding metal, the pure essence will have a beneficial effect by purifying the corruption. To demonstrate how this theory can be applied in practice, specific examples are given below.

ঔৄৎ

1. Long Term Afflictions

Case Study B - Linda

Linda, a very active person, was worried and exasperated because her deteriorating health was beginning to slow her down. The prospect of a sedate lifestyle was too much for her and she asked for help.

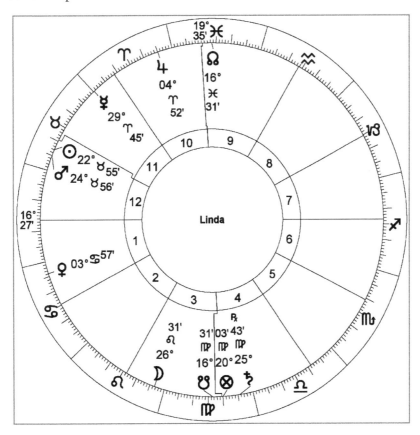

The first step was to find out about her temperament and the table below shows in detail how to do this.

		S	C	M	P
Rising Sign	Gemini	2			
Its Lord	Mercury	1			
Moon Sign	Leo		2		
Its Lord	Sun		1		
Moon Phase	2/4		1		
QAS	Autumn			2	
Sun Sign	Taurus			1	
Its Lord	Venus				1
LoG	Mars		1		
Score		3	5	3	1

The result clearly shows that the choleric temperament is dominant in Linda's chart. This matches well with the description she gave of herself. The next step was to calculate the dignities and debilities of Linda's natal planets. These are listed below.

Planet	Sign	Score
☉	22♉55	-15
☽	26♌31	1
☿	29♈45	4
♀	03♋57	24
♂	24♉56	-11
♃	04♈52	13
♄	25♏43	-5

To establish the level of dignity or debility, expressed through the positive or negative value given to any of the seven planets, we have to use the tables provided in the first part of this book. To demonstrate how dignities and debilities are calculated, I am going to describe the necessary procedure in full, below.

First we look for any mutual receptions between the planets. Here we find that the Sun is in mutual reception to Venus by term. Therefore, we give the Sun and Venus a value of +2 each. Venus is also in mutual reception with Mars by triplicity from which Venus gathers a further 3 points as does Mars.

Next we take a look at the Sun, finding that he is peregrine we deduct 5 points, and in the 12ᵗʰ house we deduct a further 5 points. The Sun is also slow so -2, and he is within 5 degrees of the malefic fixed star Algol, -5. Not forgetting to add the 2 points gained from the mutual reception with Venus, this brings the total value to -15, showing that the Sun is essentially and accidentally debilitated.

Now we continue with the Moon, who is peregrine, -5; in the third house, +1; slow, -2. She is also free of the Sun's beams, +5, and is waxing, +2. Added up, we find that the Moon's value is +1.

The same process is applied to Mercury who is peregrine, -5; located in the 11ᵗʰ house, +4; direct, +4; slow, -2; oriental, -2; free of the Sun's beams, +5. This brings it to a total value of +4, which shows that Mercury is slightly dignified.

Venus is next and she is face ruler, +1; in the 1ˢᵗ house, +5; direct, +4. She is also swift, +2; occidental, +2; free of the Sun's beams, +5. Not forgetting the +5 points from the mutual reception, we find that Venus is the strongest planet in the chart with a value of +24.

Next we take a close look at Mars, who is term ruler, +2; in his detriment, -5; in the 12ᵗʰ house, -5. He is also direct, +4; swift, +2; occidental, -2; combust, -5. We also note that Mars is within 5 degrees of the malevolent fixed star Algol, -5. Even though we can add

+3 from the mutual reception to Venus by triplicity, Mars turns out to be severely debilitated with a value of -11.

Taking a look at Jupiter next we find that he is peregrine, -5; in the 10th house, +5; direct, +4; swift, +2. Jupiter is also oriental, +2, and free of the Sun's beams, +5. This gives him a value of +13.

Lastly we evaluate Saturn, who is peregrine, -5; located in the fourth house, +4; retrograde, -5. He is also slow, -2; occidental, -2; free of the Sun's beams, +5. This adds up to a value of -5, making Saturn slightly debilitated.

Taking everything into account, we reach the conclusion that Linda's temperament is largely that of the choleric and that she has debilitated planets in her birth chart. Looking back at our description of the choleric, we find that:

> "The choleric temperament combines the primary qualities of hot and dry and is associated with the element of fire. People whose temperament is mainly choleric are enthusiastic, optimistic, assertive, often aggressive. They are always ready for action, enterprising and enthusiastic, often impatient. Typically cholerics often tend to change their mind, working on a plethora of projects. Because the choleric is primarily hot and dry, he may frequently experience a lack of experiencing deep emotions."

Knowing that both planets, Sun and Mars, are connected to the fire element and, therefore, to the choleric temperament, it must seem obvious that any debility will significantly affect the native. Turning back to the chapter describing the Sun and his corresponding gemstones, we find:

> "If the Sun is found to be essentially or accidentally afflicted in a nativity or temporarily debilitated through other influences, amber, imperial topaz (gold topaz) or ruby may be used as a remedy."

Looking at Mars in close detail, we notice that Scorpio is on the cusp of the 6th house which signifies the cause of illness and whether it is curable or not. We know that diseases of Mars are, amongst others, quick burning fevers and inflammations, measles, smallpox, ruptures of blood vessels, wounds with loss of blood. Scorpio is ruled by Mars and we have already seen that he is associated with the fire element as well as the choleric temperament. Also, a closer look at the placement of Mars shows that he is located in the 12th house signifying sorrow, envy, betrayal, affliction and self-undoing. To strengthen debilitated Mars and to try to counteract or limit the severity of all the above, we can apply the gemstones garnet, haematite, jasper or magnetite.

Linda was advised to wear one or more of the gemstones mentioned above. Here are her own words about the treatment:

> "Thank you so much, I have been wearing garnet and haematite, which are helping me feel better, less tired and able to see a treatment option I could not see before. Things are getting better, thank you again."

Case Study B – Ken, belonging to this category, can be found in the Introduction.

ॐ

2. Temporary Afflictions

Temporary afflictions can be easy to trace or they may be hidden from the view of the casual observer. Some people use Mercury stones during Mercury retrograde phases, others watch out for 'out of bounds' phases of the planets, using the appropriate gemstones to restore emotional balance. It is also of advantage to watch out for hard Saturn or Mars transits. Once these are identified, the afflicted natal planet can be strengthened with the appropriate gemstone. The next case study shows how somebody who was affected by a Saturn transit used planetary gemstones to alleviate the detrimental effect. Thereafter, I will show an examination of how the firdaria could shed light on a difficult phase in a young man's life.

Case Study C - Angelica

Angelica, a high-flying business woman, had a life-long interest in astrology and was also very fond of gemstones, particularly the expensive kind, which were often set in gold or platinum. She had developed an intuitive approach, wearing jewellery that "felt right and seemed to provide help" at certain times. Angelica approached me to find out if there was any possibility of predicting which gemstone would be most helpful in certain situations, rather than relying on her intuition alone.

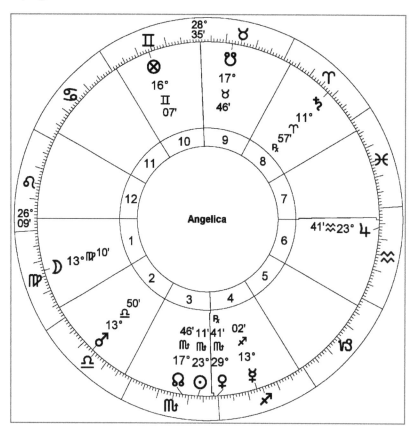

The table below shows Angelica's temperament. We can see that the melancholic temperament dominates.

		S	C	M	P
Rising Sign	Leo		2		
Its Lord	Sun		1		
Moon Sign	Virgo			2	
Its Lord	Mercury			1	
Moon Phase	4/4				1
QAS	Autumn			2	
Sun Sign	Scorpio			1	
Its Lord	Mars	1			
LoG	Mercury			1	
Score		1	3	7	1

Looking at the strengths and weaknesses of Angelica's natal planets, we realise that her Saturn, her Venus and her Sun are debilitated.

Planet	Sign	Score
☉	23♏11	-2
☽	13♏10	13
☿	13♐02	17
♀	29♏41ʀ	-5
♂	13♎50	11
♃	23♒41	11
♄	11♈57ʀ	-11

Angelica's knowledge of astrology enabled her to establish when hard transits, particularly those involving Saturn or Mars, would take place in her life. All she needed to know was which precious stone she needed to wear to counteract the effects of these transits. Two examples will be sufficient to demonstrate the underlying pattern. Between 2000 and 2001, transiting Saturn was opposing Angelica's natal Venus three times. When transiting Saturn is opposing natal Venus, it is generally interpreted as a time of worry, grief or general sadness. Angelica's Venus is located in the 4th house with Taurus, her sign of rulership in a nocturnal chart, on the 10th house cusp. This shows that during this transit she could expect a troublesome time in connection with her parents. At the time the transits took place, Angelica was in her early 60s and it was likely that illness or even the death of one of her parents might occur. To help overcome this time of potential sadness, Angelica wore an emerald ring she had in her possession. Aquamarine or heliotrope would also have been ideal to counteract Saturn's influence on her Venus. During 2006 and 2007, transiting Saturn was opposing Angelica's natal Jupiter. Her Jupiter is close to the 7th house cusp and Pisces, his nocturnal sign of rulership, is on the cusp of the 8th house. Transiting Saturn opposing Jupiter is generally considered to be a troublesome time for finances. The placement of Jupiter in the birth chart suggests the danger of business related difficulties, particularly if a business partner is involved. If not taken care of, this could lead to financial worries. To strengthen Jupiter who was temporarily afflicted by Saturn's opposition, amethyst, sapphire, topaz or zircon should be worn.

৵৽৹

Case Study D - Martin

I was approached by his grandmother when Martin was 18 years of age. She wrote that she was becoming very worried about Martin, because "in the past months he has been very anxious and depressed". She also added that he told her that he felt as if "his heart was full of holes". Martin's natal chart is reproduced below.

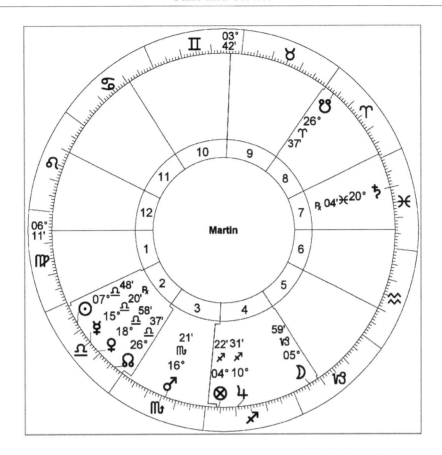

The first step was to find out if Martin's temperament could shed any light on the reasons for his anxiety and depression.

		S	C	M	P
Rising Sign	Virgo			2	
Its Lord	Mercury			1	
Moon Sign	Sagittarius		2		
Its Lord	Saturn			1	
Moon Phase	1/4	1			
QAS	Autumn			2	
Sun Sign	Libra	1			
Its Lord	Venus				1
LoG	Jupiter	1			
Score		3	2	6	1

From these calculations it is obvious that Martin's temperament is predominantly that of the melancholic. Looking back at the chapter on the melancholic temperament, we recall "melancholics are generally very patient but their rigidity, due to the cold quality, can make them pessimistic, melancholic and even depressed". We also know that the planet connected with the melancholic temperament is Saturn. In Part 1, we stated that "Saturn is also known as the *Greater Malefic*, or the *Greater Infortune*, connected with fear, envy and hatred". Thus, Martin has a natural predisposition to melancholia, anxiety and depression. We also notice that Saturn is the ruler of Aquarius, the sign on the 6th house cusp. Saturn is located in the 7th house; in other words, Martin will always be strongly affected by the fate of others around him. To find out more details, we have to look closely at the strengths and weaknesses of his natal planets.

Planet	Sign	Score
☉	07♎48	-4
☽	05♑59	13
☿	15♎20ℝ	2
♀	18♎58	18
♂	16♏21	18
♃	10♐31	22
♄	20♓04ℝ	3

From the table above, we can see that the Sun, peregrine and in his fall, is Martin's weakest planet. To counteract this weakness, it would be beneficial for him to wear amber, gold topaz or ruby. Martin's natal Saturn is peregrine and retrograde, but otherwise not in bad condition and rather well placed. It also seemed that his spell of anxiety and depression was rather more temporary than prolonged. To find an explanation and to reduce the duration of this phase of depression as much as possible, I considered his firdaria. This is a traditional astrological technique, attributed to the Persians where a person's life is divided into unequal parts attributed to the rulership of different planets. The sequence of this division of the firdaria is different for diurnal or nocturnal nativities. As Martin's birth chart is nocturnal, I give the sequence for nocturnal births, below.

Moon - 9 years, Saturn - 11 years, Jupiter - 12 years, Mars - 7 years, Sun - 10 years, Venus - 8 years, Mercury -13 years, North Node - 3 years, South Node - 2 years.

These firdaria are usually subdivided and the duration of each subdivision is found by dividing the period of the firdar's main planet by seven. Thus we find the firdar of the Moon subdivided into Moon/Moon, Moon/Saturn, Moon/Jupiter, Moon/Mars, Moon/Sun, Moon/Venus and Moon/Mercury. Thereafter the sequence continues with Saturn/Saturn, Saturn/Jupiter, Saturn/Mars, Saturn/Sun, Saturn/Venus, Saturn/Mercury and Saturn/Moon.

In Martin's case, we can see that being 18 years of age, he had completed his Moon firdar and was coming to the end of his Saturn firdar. In fact, at the time his grandmother wrote to me, he was in the last months of his Saturn/Moon firdar. From the sequence above, we can see that his next firdar was going to be Jupiter/Jupiter. A quick look at our table above shows that Martin's Jupiter is highly dignified, and it was therefore likely that his problems of anxiety and depression would recede. At the present time though, he was obviously suffering from a surplus of saturnine influences of his melancholic temperament and the temporary affliction through the Saturn/Moon firdar. Whilst waiting for the Jupiter/Jupiter firdar to come into effect, I decided to counteract the Greater Malefic's force with gemstones corresponding to Jupiter, the Greater Benefic. These gemstones are amethyst, topaz, sapphire or zircon.

3. Talismans

Case Study E – Christopher

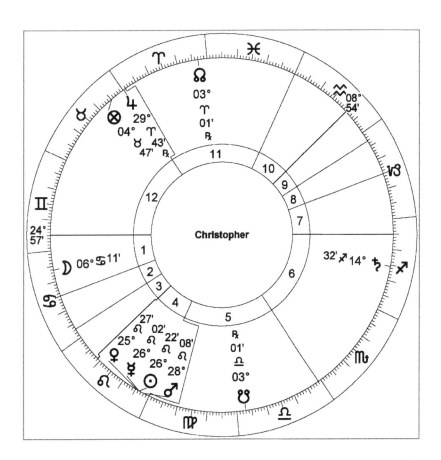

Christopher, an artist who was in his early 30s at the time of the consultation, contacted me because he had "been struggling with trying to merge opposite tendencies". He also wrote that his "all or nothing attitude has been sorely noted by my friends and family".

		S	C	M	P
Rising Sign	Gemini	2			
Its Lord	Mercury	1			
Moon Sign	Cancer				2
Its Lord	Cancer				1
Moon Phase	4/4				1
QAS	Summer		2		
Sun	Leo		1		
Its Lord	Sun		1		
LoG	Mercury	1			
Score		4	4	0	4

A look at Christopher's temperament shows that the sanguine, choleric, and melancholic temperament are present in equal measure. We have seen that those whose temperament is mainly choleric are enthusiastic, optimistic, assertive, often aggressive. They are always ready for action, are enterprising and enthusiastic and often impatient. The typically phlegmatic type, on the other hand, is sensitive with a strong emotional emphasis and tends to be quite inconsistent, often subjective with an element of laziness. Christopher agreed that this was the case and that he was, in his own words, "very much struggling between opposite tendencies in my life; struggling between the extrovert and the introvert, activity and laziness". His question therefore was if "it would be wise to try and live and possibly reconcile both rather than trying to suppress the one over the other?" We know that the choleric temperament consists of the primary qualities hot and dry, represented by Mars and the Sun. The phlegmatic temperament consists of the primary qualities cold and wet, represented by the Moon.

Planet	Sign	Score
☉	26♌22	6
☽	06♋11	13
☿	26♌02	-3
♀	25♌27	-3
♂	28♌08	5
♃	29♈43ᴿ	-2
♄	14♐32	-2

Christopher's planetary dignities and debilities show that his Sun, Mars and Moon are all in good condition. To find a way to try to reconcile the opposing forces of the choleric and the phlegmatic temperament, we have to emphasise the middle ground. In this case, we tried to strengthen Venus, the planet of equilibrium and balance. We can see from Christopher's table of planetary dignities and debilities that Venus is also slightly debilitated, in which case the use of a Venus gemstone is even more justifiable. Christopher, who also has a background in ritual magic, expressed an interest in creating a Venus talisman with a Venus stone in the centre. Using his artistic abilities, Christopher designed his Venus talisman, shown below. The most auspicious time to create and consecrate the talisman was established by the rules of electional astrology and Christopher carried out the construction and subsequent consecration at the appropriate day and hour.

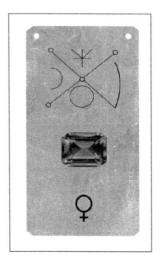

4. Fixed Star Rings

Another method to use the power of gemstones and crystals is the creation of fixed star rings. As a result of their beneficial properties, these are sometimes known as "lucky rings". In the first book of his *De Occulta Philosophia*, the German occultist Agrippa von Nettesheim devotes a whole chapter to the principal rules of making fixed star rings. He writes:

> "The way how these rings are made is as follows: When a fortunate star is rising and is looked upon by the Moon in a fortunate way, or is in conjunction to the Moon, we have to take a stone and a herb which are corresponding to the star; then we have to make a ring out of the metal corresponding to the star and, after we have placed the herb or root below the stone, fix the it to the ring. Lastly, engravings of pictures, names and characters, as well as suffumigations should not be omitted."

Translated into modern English, this means that for the successful creation of a fixed star ring, a few rules have to be observed. Firstly, the fixed star has to be rising, i.e. it has to be conjunct the Ascendant. Some sources also allow the fixed star to be conjunct the midheaven. Secondly, the Moon has to be in an applying conjunction, trine or sextile to the fixed star. I would recommend finding an election with a tight conjunction to achieve best results. Thirdly, the Moon and the fixed star should not be afflicted. This means specifically that there should be no applying conjunctions between the fixed star or the Moon and Saturn or Mars. Also disallowed are applying oppositions or squares to any other planet or the south lunar node. It is also of importance to make sure that neither the fixed star nor the Moon is combust (that is within 8.5 degrees of the Sun). Lastly, the Moon should be in her waxing phase. The fixed stars Agrippa mentions are also known as the Fifteen Fortunate Stars or Behenian stars. Details of these are given below.

The Fifteen Fortunate Stars:

1. **Algol**, also known as **Caput Algol**: This fixed star, marking the Medusa's Head held in the hand of Perseus, is currently located at 26 degrees Taurus. It promises boldness and victory, gives success to petitions, and turns spells back against the person who cast them. The corresponding gemstone is the diamond. Black hellebore and mugwort are Algol's corresponding herbs. Algol's sigil is:

2. **Pleiades**: These seven sister-stars, one of which is invisible, are currently located in the neighbourhood of 29 degrees Taurus. They are said to sharpen the sense of vision, and also to reveal secret and hidden things. Their corresponding gemstone is crystal. Fennel and the herb Diacedon are their corresponding plants. The sigil of the Pleiades is

3. **Aldebaran** or **Aldaboram**: This fixed star, which is one of the four Royal Stars, is currently located at 9 degrees Gemini. Aldebaran is said that it increases riches, honour and glory. Its corresponding gemstone is the ruby. Spurge (euphorbia sp.) and woodruff are Aldebaran's corresponding herbs. Aldebaran's sigil is

4. Capella, also known as **Alhayhoch** or **Hircus**: This fixed star, situated in the body of the Goat in the arms of Auriga, is currently located at 21 degrees Gemini. It helps towards honours and ensures the help of princes. It is also said to be good against toothache. Capella's corresponding gemstone is the sapphire. Corresponding herbs are horehound (Marrubium vulgare), mint and mugwort. Capella's sigil is

5. Sirius, also known as **Canis major**: This fixed star, situated in the mouth of the Greater Dog, is currently located at 14 degrees Cancer. It grants the goodwill and favour of men and airy spirits. Its corresponding gemstone is beryl. Sirius' corresponding herbs are savine (Juniperus sabina), mugwort and dracontea or dragonwort (Artemisia dracunculus). The sigil of Sirius is

6. Procyon (Canis minor): This fixed star, situated in the body of the Lesser Dog, is currently located at 25 degrees Cancer. It bestows favour of gods, spirits and men, and preserves one's health. The corresponding gemstone is agate. Procyon's corresponding plants are heliotrope and pennyroyal. Procyon's sigil is

7. Regulus (Cor Leonis): This fixed star, situated in the body of the Lion, is the second of the four Royal Stars. Currently, Regulus is located at 00 degrees Virgo. This fixed star is said to repress melancholy and to make a man temperate and agreeable. Regulus' corresponding gemstone is the garnet. The corresponding herb is swalloword (which is possibly Chelidonium majus). The sigil of Regulus is

8. **Alkaid (Cauda Ursae)**: This fixed star, situated in the Bear's tail, is currently located at 27 degrees Virgo. Alkaid is said to provide protection from robbers and poison. It also protects travellers. Alkaid's corresponding gemstone is the loadstone. Its corresponding herbs are chicory and mugwort. Alkaid's sigil is

9. **Gienah (Ala Corvi)**: This fixed star, situated in the right wing of the Crow, is currently located at 13 degrees Libra. It is said that Gienah increases boldness and drives away evil spirits. It also protects from winds and the malice of men. Gienah's corresponding gemstone is black onyx. Its corresponding herbs are sorrel, henbane, comfrey and frog tongue (Sedum sp.). Gienah's sigil is

10. **Spica**: This fixed star, situated in the Wheat Ear of Virgo, is currently located at 23 degrees Libra. It increases riches and victory and releases from poverty. Spica's corresponding gemstone is the emerald. Its corresponding plants are sage, trefoil, mandrake and mugwort. Spica's sigil is

11. **Arcturus (Alchameth)**: This fixed star, situated on the left knee of Boötis, is currently located at 24 degrees Libra. It strengthens the blood and expels fevers. Arcturus' corresponding gemstone is jasper and its corresponding herb is plantain. Arcturus' sigil is

12. **Alphecca (Elpheia)**: This fixed star, situated in the knot of the ribbon in the Corona Borealis, is currently located at 12 degrees Scorpio. The fixed star is said to bestow grace,

chastity and glory. Its corresponding gemstone is the topaz. Alphecca's corresponding plants are rosemary, trefoil and ivy. Alphecca's sigil is

13. **Antares (Cor scorpii)**: This fixed star, situated in the body of the Scorpion is the third of the four Royal Stars. It is currently located at 19 degrees Sagittarius. It is said to give understanding and memory. Antares also drives out evil spirits. Its corresponding gemstones are sardonyx and amethyst. Its corresponding plants are long birthwort and saffron. The sigil of Antares is

14. **Vega (Vultur cadens)**: This fixed star, situated in the lower part of the Lyre, is currently located at 15 degrees Capricorn. It is said to make the wearer temperate, magnanimous and proud. Vega's corresponding gemstone is the chrysolithe. Its corresponding herbs are succory (Cychorium intybus) and fumitary. Vega's sigil is

15. **Deneb Algedi (Cauda Capricorni)**: This fixed star, situated in the tail of the Goat, is currently located at 23 degrees Aquarius. It is said that it furnishes favour in lawsuits, increases wealth and makes men and their homes safe. Vega's corresponding gemstone is the chalcedony. Marjoram, catnip, mugwort and mandrake are its corresponding plants. Deneb Algedi's sigil is

Case Study F - Creation of a Fixed Star Ring

To create a lucky ring, the first step towards this goal must be to undertake an astrological election which will determine the most auspicious moment to act, fixing the attributes of the beneficial star to the ring. In our example, we want to ensure the goodwill and favour of men and airy spirits. For this purpose we aim to create a Sirius ring. Knowing that Sirius is located in 14 degrees Cancer, we try to find a date and time when the fixed star will be conjunct the Ascendant in our chosen location. Once this is achieved, we have to try and fulfil the other rules we have stated above. The chart below shows the result of the election.

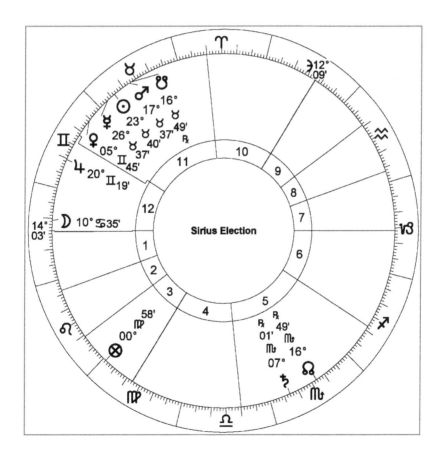

Following the rules, we find that on 14 May 2013 at 08:26 am, Sirius is conjunct the Ascendant at 14 degrees Cancer. The Moon is in an applying conjunction to Sirius. We can also see that the Moon is not afflicted. Having left the conjunction, she is applying to the Sun by sextile, and is in her waxing phase. Having fulfilled all the necessary criteria, we have elected the perfect time to create a Sirius ring.

The next step is to physically create the fixed star ring. Here we have two possibilities. We can either purchase a ready-made beryl ring, or we can order a blank ring and a beryl cabochon of our choice. We will also need a diamond tipped stylus to engrave the corresponding sigil onto the gemstone. A portion of the corresponding plant or herb will also be needed. This is not the place to describe the details of the ritual activity surrounding the creation of the fixed star ring, as this will differ according to individual preference. There are a few basic tasks, though, which should be carried out carefully and in the order given here. First of all, the sigil has to be inscribed onto the stone. If the gemstone is already set into the ring, the sigil will need to be inscribed onto the top surface but if the stone is loose, the sigil can be scratched onto the side that will be glued onto the ring. The next step is to apply the herb or herb-mixture. If the ring is ready-made, it should be immersed in a strong solution made from the corresponding herbs. If the stone and the ring were purchased separately, the herb, or herb-mixture, should be mixed into the glue that is used to fix the stone to the setting. Once the ring has been engraved and immersed, or engraved and assembled, the intent should be stated. This may be done in the form of an invocation. Thereafter the ring should be moved through incense smoke to conclude the consecration.

ॐॐ

5. Planetary and Constellational Images

Not only seals of fixed stars, but also images connected with planets and constellations can be engraved onto gemstones to enhance their virtues. The concept behind this method is similar to the one we encountered in the chapter above. The selected image is engraved onto a corresponding stone at the moment the appropriate planet or constellation is either rising (i.e. conjunct the ascendant), or in a strong house position.

The following descriptions of images and virtues are drawn from Leonardi's *Speculum Lapidum*, first published in Venice, 1502.

Images of Planets

Saturn: The image of Saturn is that of an old man, holding a curved scythe in his hand; he has a small beard. Engraved on a stone of Saturn's nature, it renders the wearer powerful and continually augments his power.

Jupiter: The image of Jupiter is that of a seated figure, sometimes in a chariot, holding a staff in one hand and a spear in the other. It renders the wearer fortunate, especially engraved on a Kabratis stone. He easily gains what he wishes for, particularly from priests. He will be raised to honours and dignities. (Kabratis, also kabrates, was thought to be crystal).

Mars: The image used for Mars is sometimes a banner and sometimes a lance or another weapon. He is, indeed, always armed and, at times, mounted on a horse. It gives victory, boldness in war, and success in everything, especially if engraved on an appropriate stone.

Venus: Many different images, amongst them that of a woman with a voluminous dress and a stole, holding a laurel in her hand. It gives skill in handling affairs and usually brings them to a successful end. It also removes the fear of drowning.

Mercury: The image used is that of a slender man, usually with a beautiful beard, but sometimes without. He has winged feet and holds a caduceus. It increases knowledge and confers eloquence. It also aids merchants, enabling them to acquire wealth.

Sun: The image used is a solar disk with rays, sometimes a man in a chariot, occasionally surrounded by the signs of the zodiac. It renders the wearer powerful and makes him a victor. This gem is also highly prized by hunters.

Moon: Various images can be used, sometimes it is a crescent Moon, and at times it is a young woman in a chariot, holding a quiver. At other times, a young woman with a quiver, following the chase with dogs. It aids the fortune of those who are sent on an embassy, and enables them to acquire wealth and honour in the process. It is also said to confer speed and facility in undertakings and a happy result.

ॐ

Images of Constellations

The information about images and use of the following constellations is based on material found in Camilli Leonardi's *Speculum Lapidum*.

Ara (Sacrarius Turubulus): This constellation is also known as the Altar. Its image is that of an altar with lit incense. Its nature is that of Venus and Mercury. It gives the wearer the power to recognise spirits, to converse with them and to command them. It also confers chastity. Ara is a southern constellation currently located between 17 degrees Sagittarius and 4 degrees Capricorn.

Andromeda: This constellation is also known as the Chained Woman. Its image is that of a young girl with dishevelled hair her hands hanging down. Its nature is that of Venus. It reconciles husband and wife, strengthens love, and protects the human body from many diseases. Andromeda is a northern constellation currently located between 2 degrees Aries and 25 degrees Taurus.

Aquila: This constellation is also known as the Eagle. Its image is that of a flying eagle with an arrow beneath its feet. It nature is that of Jupiter and Mercury. The nature of the arrow is of Mars and Venus. It preserves former honours, adds new ones and helps to gain victory. Aquila is a northern constellation currently located between 17 degrees Capricorn and 5 degrees Aquarius.

Auriga: This constellation is also known as the Charioteer. Its image is that of a man in a chariot bearing a goat on his left shoulder. Its nature is that of Mercury and it makes the wearer successful in hunting. Auriga is a northern constellation currently located between 13 degrees Gemini and 19 degrees Cancer.

Canis Major: This constellation is also known as the Greater Dog. Its image is that of a dog for coursing hares; it has a curved tail. Its nature is that of Venus and it cures lunacy, insanity and daemonic possession. Canis Major is a southern constellation currently located between 3 degrees Cancer and 2 degrees Leo.

Canis Minor: This constellation is also known as the Lesser Dog. Its image is that of a sitting dog. Its nature is that of Jupiter and it guards from dropsy, pestilence and dog bites. Canis Minor is a southern constellation currently located between 18 degrees Cancer and 8 degrees Leo.

Cassiopeia: This constellation is also known as the Queen. Its image is that of a woman seated in a chair with her hands extended in the form of a cross. Sometimes she has a triangle on her head. Its nature is that of Saturn and Venus. It restores a sickly, worn body to health, gives quiet and calm after labour and procures pleasant and tranquil sleep. Cassiopeia is a northern constellation currently located between 16 degrees Aries and 17 degrees Gemini.

Centaurus: This constellation is also known as the Centaur. Its image is that of a half-figure of a bull bearing a man on whose shoulder rests a lance from which depends a hare. In his right hand, the man holds a small, supine animal with a vessel attached to it. Its nature is that of Jupiter and Mars. It provides constancy and perpetual health. Centaurus is a southern constellation currently located between 4 degrees Libra and 1 degree Sagittarius.

Cepheus: This constellation is also known as the King. Its image is that of a man girt with a sword holding his arms and hands extended. Its nature is that of Saturn and Jupiter. It causes pleasant visions if placed beneath the head of a sleeping person. Cepheus is a northern constellation currently located from 18 degrees Pisces throughout Aries, Taurus and Libra, to 7 degrees Cancer.

Cetus: This constellation is also known as the Sea Monster, or Whale. Its depiction is that of a large fish with a curved tail and a capacious gullet. Its nature is that of Saturn. It makes the wearer fortunate on the sea and makes him prudent and agreeable. It also restores lost articles. Cetus is a southern constellation currently located between 18 degrees Pisces and 21 degrees Taurus.

Corona Australis: This constellation is also known as the Southern Crown. Its depiction is that of an imperial crown. Its nature is that of Saturn and Mars. It augments wealth and makes the wearer a happy person. Corona Australis is a southern constellation currently located between 0 degrees Capricorn and 16 degrees Capricorn.

Corona Borealis: This constellation is also known as the Northern Crown. Its depiction is that of a crown with many stars and sometimes the crowned head of a king. Its nature is that of Venus and Mercury. Engraved on the stone of one who is fitted for honours and knowledge, it gives him great favour with rulers. Corona Borealis is a northern constellation currently located between 3 degrees Scorpio and 29 degrees Scorpio.

Cygnus: This constellation is also known as the Swan. Its depiction is that of a swan with outstretched wings and a curved neck. Its nature is that of Venus and Mercury. It makes the wearer popular, increases knowledge and augments wealth. It also cures gout, paralysis and fever. Cygnus is a northern constellation currently located from 28 degrees Capricorn throughout Aquarius, Pisces to 8 degrees Aries.

Delphinus: This constellation is also known as the Dolphin. Its depiction is omitted in *Speculum Lapidum*, but it is likely to be that of a dolphin, which, according to Leonardi, should be depicted in relief. Its nature is that of Saturn and Mars. If the engraved gem is attached to nets, it causes them to be filled with fish and it renders the wearer fortunate in fishing. Delphinus is a northern constellation currently located between 9 degrees Aquarius and 25 degrees Aquarius.

Hercules: This constellation is also known as the Kneeling Man, or the Strong Man. Its image is that of a man with bent knees holding a club in his hand and killing a lion. Sometimes it is a man with a lion skin in his hand or over his shoulder holding a club. Its nature is that of Venus and Mercury. Engraved on a stone that brings victory, like agate, it renders the wearer victorious in all conflicts in the field. Hercules is a northern constellation currently located from 25 degrees Libra, throughout Sagittarius to 19 degrees Capricorn.

Hydra: This constellation is also known as the Water-Snake. Its image is that of a serpent having an urn at its head and a raven at its tail. Its nature is that of Saturn and Venus. It brings riches and all good gifts to the wearer making him cautious and prudent. Hydra is a southern constellation currently located between 7 degrees Leo, throughout Virgo, Libra, and 22 degrees Scorpio.

Lepus: This constellation is also known as the Hare. Its image is that of the figure of a hare with its ears pricked up. The feet are represented as if in swift motion. Its nature is that of Saturn and Mercury. It cures frenzy and protects from the wiles of daemons. Whoever wears this cannot be hurt by a malignant spirit. Lepus is a southern constellation currently located between 6 degrees Gemini and 3 degrees Cancer.

Navis, or Argo Navis: This constellation is also known as the Great Ship. Its image is that of a ship with prow curved back and spread sails. Sometimes it is depicted with, sometimes without, oars. Its nature is that of Saturn and Jupiter. It renders the wearer fortunate in his undertakings, neither does he run any risk on sea or water, nor can he be injured by water. Navis is a southern constellation, currently located between 2 degrees Cancer and 24 degrees Scorpio.

Orion: This constellation is also known as the Great Hunter. Its image is that of a man with or without armour holding a scythe or a sword in his hand. Its nature is that of Saturn, Jupiter and Mars and it gives the wearer victory over his enemies. Orion is a southern constellation currently located between 9 degrees Gemini and 6 degrees Cancer.

Pegasus: This constellation is also known as the Flying Horse. Its image is that of half a winged horse. Others depict the whole figure omitting the bridle. Its nature is that of Mars and Jupiter. It gives victory in the field and makes the wearer swift, cautious and bold. Pegasus is a northern constellation currently located between 24 degrees Aquarius, throughout Pisces, and 15 degrees Aries.

Perseus: This constellation is also known as the Champion or Hero. Its image is that of a man holding a sword in his right hand and the Gorgon's head in his left. Its nature is that of Saturn and Venus. It guards the wearer from misfortune and protects not only the wearer, but also the place where it may be, from lightning and tempest. It also dissolves enchantments. Perseus is a northern constellation, currently located between 12 degrees Taurus and 20 degrees Gemini.

Serpens: This constellation is also known as the Serpent. Its image is that of a man in the folds of a serpent holding its head in his right and its tail in his left hand. Its nature is that of Saturn and Venus. It is an antidote to poisons and to the bites of venomous creatures. Serpens is a northern constellation currently split into Serpens Caput, located between 13 degrees Scorpio and 4 degrees Sagittarius, and Serpens Cauda, located between 29 degrees Sagittarius and 16 degrees Capricorn.

Ursa Major, Ursa Minor and Draco: Ursa Major is also known as the Great Bear, Ursa Minor as the Little Bear, and Draco as the Dragon. Leonardi does not provide us with images, but writes that Ursa Major is of the nature of Mars and Venus. Ursa Minor is of the nature of Saturn. Draco is of the nature of Saturn and Mars. They render the wearer wise, cautious, versatile and powerful. These are all northern constellations. Ursa Major is currently located from 14 degrees Cancer, throughout Leo, Virgo to 3 degrees Libra. Ursa Minor is currently located from 23 degrees Gemini, throughout Cancer, Leo to 19 degrees Virgo. Draco is a circumpolar constellation.

Vexillum (Vela): This constellation is also known as the Sail. Its image is that of a flag flying from the top of a lance. Although not mentioned by Leonardi, we can assume that its nature is that of Saturn and Jupiter as it is part of Navis (see above). It provides skill in war and confers victory in the field. Vela is a southern constellation currently located between 21 degrees Leo and 22 degrees Libra.

APPENDICES

Therapeutic Index

Anaemia: Lapis lazuli, Jupiter

Anxiety, help against: Coral, Sun

Allergies: Pearl, Moon

Anorexia: Imperial topaz, Sun

Antidepressant: Spinel, Sun; lapis lazuli, Jupiter

Antispasmodic: Zircon, Jupiter

Appetite, increasing of: Ruby, Sun

Appetite, loss of: Topaz, Jupiter; imperial topaz, Sun

Assertiveness, increasing of: Peridot, Mercury

Asthma: Zircon, Jupiter

Belly ache: Rock crystal, Moon

Bladder problems: Haematite, Mars

Blood pressure, lowering of: Lapis lazuli, Jupiter

Blood circulation, improvement of: Ruby, Sun

Blood cleansing: Ruby, Sun

Blood disorders: Topaz, Jupiter

Blood, stop flowing out of wounds: Haematite, carnelian, Mars

Brain activity, increase of: Turquoise, Mercury

Breast milk: Jasper, Mars

Bronchial problems: Zircon, Jupiter

Bruises: Amethyst, Jupiter

Calmness, restoration of: Turquoise, Mercury

Childbirth: Haematite, Mars

Communication, enhanced ability of: Peridot, Mercury

Cough: Agate, Mercury

Courage, increase levels of: Carnelian, Mars

Creativity, increase of: Opal, Mercury

Danger, protection from: Coral, Sun

Deafness: Agate, Mercury

Depression: Coral, Sun, garnet, Mars; jet, Saturn

Detox: Beryl, copper chalcedony, heliotrope, Venus

Ears, problems with: Agate, Mercury

Epilepsy: Selenite, Moon

Evil eye: Coral, Sun

Eyes, diseases of: Green agate, Mercury

Eyesight, problems with: Beryl, Venus

Fear, transformation into optimism: Black opal, Mercury

Fertility, increasing of: Selenite, Moon

Fever: Rock crystal, Moon; Sapphire, Jupiter

Focusing attention: Black onyx, Saturn

Friendship, create and strengthen: Peridot, Mercury

Fungal infection: Black onyx, Saturn

Gastritis: Agate, Mercury

Grief, overcoming of: Jet, Saturn

Grounding effect: Black onyx, Saturn

Hallucinations, disappearance of: ruby, Sun

Headache: Amethyst, Jupiter

Healing, increased: Sapphire, Jupiter

Heart problems: Sapphire, Jupiter, rock crystal, Moon

Hope, promotion of: Garnet, Mars

Hyperactivity, balancing of: Ruby, Sun

Illusions, getting rid of: Peridot, Mercury

Immune system, boosting of: Heliotrope, Venus; garnet, Mars

Infectious diseases: Ruby, Sun

Inflammation, general prevention: Black onyx, Saturn; heliotrope, Venus

Inflammation of women's sexual organs: Copper chalcedony, Venus

Inner eye, strengthening of: Opal, Mercury

Insomnia: Spinel, Sun

Intestinal diseases: Sapphire, Jupiter

Irritability: Amber, Sun

Joy, increased levels of: Spinel, Sun

Labour, support: Magnetite, Mars

Life force, enhancing: Imperial topaz, Sun

Lethargy, diminishing of: Jasper, Mars

Liver problems, with: Magnetite, Mars

Liver, stimulation: Beryl, Venus; zircon, Jupiter

Lungs, problems with: Topaz, zircon; amethyst, Jupiter

Lymphatic system, unblocking of: Moonstone, Moon

Memorising, increased ability of: Opal, Mercury

Menopause, problems with: Moonstone, Moon; pearl, Moon

Menstrual problems, regulation of: Moonstone, Moon; jasper, Mars

Metabolism, strengthening: Imperial topaz, Sun

Mind, balanced state of: Blue lace agate, Mercury

Mind, stimulation of: Yellow agate, Mercury

Negativity: Jet, Saturn

Nightmares, prevention of: Coral, Sun

Numbness: Rock crystal, Moon

Peace and joy: Topaz, Jupiter

Poisoning: Heliotrope, turquoise, Venus

Poisonous insects: Turquoise, Venus

Potency problems: Garnet, Mars

Pregnancy: Selenite, Moon

Psychic abilities, increase of: Opal, Mercury

Rejuvenating properties: Ruby, Sun

Relaxation: Gold topaz, Sun

Respiratory tract, problems with: Amethyst, zircon, Jupiter

Revitalizing: Rock crystal, Moon

Self confidence, increase of: Beryl, Venus; garnet, Mars; peridot, Mercury

Self realisation: Gold topaz, Sun

Sexual activities, stimulating of: Ruby, Sun

Sexual attractiveness, enhancing of: Black opal, Mercury; magnetite, Mars

Sexual balance, restoring of: Garnet, Mars

Skin conditions: Pearl, Moon

Skin disorders: Black onyx, Saturn

Sleep, enhancing of: Magnetite, Mars; ruby, Sun

Sorrows: Spinel, Sun

Speaking in public: Agate, Mercury

Speech disorder: Agate, Mercury

Speech impediment: Agate, Mercury

Spiritual experiences: Zircon, Jupiter

Stimulating effects: Zircon, Jupiter

Stomach function increased: Ruby, Sun

Stomach pain: Rock crystal, Moon

Stomach problems: Moonstone, pearl, Moon; turquoise, Mercury

Stomach ulcers: Agate, Mercury

Swellings: Amethyst, Jupiter; magnetite, Mars

Styptic qualities: Haematite, magnetite, carnelian, Mars

Tension, eased: Gold topaz, Sun

Throat, problems with: Agate, Mercury

Thyroid gland, regulation: Lapis lazuli, Jupiter

Tiredness: Spinel, Sun

Tongue, problems with: Agate, Mercury

Toothache, problems with: Rock crystal, Moon

Wishes, realisation of: Blue opal, Mercury

Wounds, healing of: Garnet, Mars; amber, Sun

Tables of Fixed Star Correspondences

The table below shows fixed star, gemstone, and plant correspondences, according to Gower's, *Confessio Amantis*, book 7:

Fixed Star	Gemstone	Plant
Aldeboran (sic)	Carbuncle	Anabulla
Clota or Pliades	Crystal	Fennel
Algol	Diamond	Black hellebore
Alhaiot	Sapphire	Horehound
Greater Dog Star	Beryl	Savin
Lesser Dog Star	Agate	Cowslip
Arial	Gorgonza	Celandine
Crow's Wing	Honochinus	Sorrel
Alaezel	Emerald	Sage
Almareth	Jasper	Plantain
Venenas	Adamant	Chicory
Alpheta	Topaz	Rosemary
Scorpion's Heart	Sardis	Birthwort
Botercadent	Chrysolite	Savory
Scorpion's Tail	Chalcedony	Marjoram

꧁꧂

The following is a tabulation of the information given in Marsilio Ficino's *Three Books on Life**, book three, chapter 8, *Concerning the Powers and Use of the Fixed Stars:*

	Zodiacal Position*	Fixed Star	Planetary Correspondence	Crystal/ Gemstone	Plant/ Herb	Desired Effect
1	22nd degree of Aries	Navel of Andromeda	Mercurial and Veneral			
2	18th degree of Taurus	Algol	Saturn and Jupiter	diamond	mugwort	Boldness and victory
3	22nd degree of Taurus	Pleiades	Lunar and Martial	crystal	diacedon, fennel-seed	Sharpens the sense of vision
4	1st or 3rd degree of Gemini	Aldebaran	Martial and Venereal	ruby	spurge, woodruff	Increases riches and glory
5	13th degree of Gemini	The Goat	Jovial and Saturnine	sapphire	Hore-hound, mint, mugwort, mandrake	Helps towards honour and the help of princes
6	6th or 7th degree of Cancer	Canis Major	Venereal	beryl	savine, mugwort, dracontea	It proffers favour
7	17th degree of Cancer	Canis Minor	Mercurial and Martial	agate	heliotrope, pennyroyal	bestows favour
8	21st degree of Leo	Heart of the Lion	A royal Jovial and Martial star	garnet	Swallow-wort, mastic	Represses melancholy and makes temperate and agreeable

9	19th degree of Virgo	Tail of Ursa Major	Venereal and Lunar	magnet	chicory, mugwort	Provides protection from robbers and poison
10	7th degree of Libra	Right Wing of the Raven				
11	12th or 13th degree of Libra	Left Wing of the Raven	Saturnine and Martial		sorrel, henbane, frog's tongue	Increases boldness and will be noxious
12	15th or 16th degree of Libra	Spica	Venereal and Mercurial	emerald	sage, trefoil, promarulla, mugwort, mandrake	Increases riches, and victory and releases from poverty
	17th or 18th degree of Libra	Alchameth		jasper	plantain	Strengthens the blood and expels fevers
13	4th degree of Scorpio	Elpheia	Venereal and Martial			
	According to another computation in the 5th degree of Scorpio	Cornea (maybe the same as above)		topaz	rosemary, trefoil and ivy	Increases grace, chastity and glory
14	3rd degree of Sagittarius	Heart of the Scorpion	Martial and Jovial	sardonyx, amethyst	long birthwort, saffron	Makes the colour good, the mind happy and

						wise and drives out daemons
15	7th degree of Capricorn	Falling Vulture	Mercurial and Venerial	chrysolite	savory, fumitory	Temperate; beneficial when in ASC or MC
16	16th degree of Aquarius	Tail of Capricorn	Saturnine and Mercurial	chalcedony	marjoram, catnip, mugwort and mandrake	Furnishes favour in lawsuits, increases wealth and makes men and their homes safe
17	3rd degree of Pisces	Shoulder of the Horse	Jovial and Martial			

*Positions of fixed stars are correct for the time Ficino published De Vita in 1489

Planetary Glyphs in Agrippa's *Three Books on Occult Philosophy*

Saturn

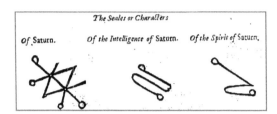

Jupiter

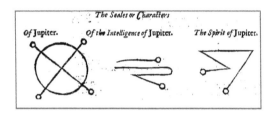

Mercury

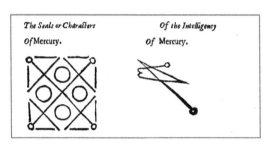

Mars

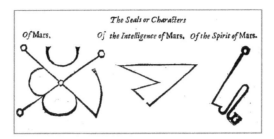

Venus

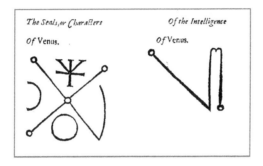

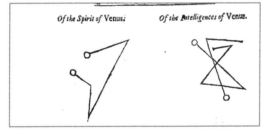

Sun

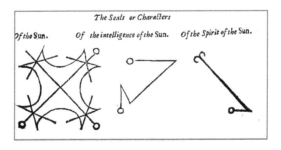

Moon

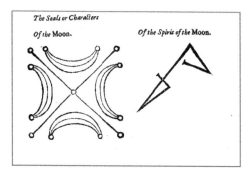

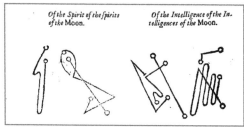

Glossary

Ascendant
The sign, but often also the particular degree of the sign, rising at the eastern horizon is called the ascendant. It is also the cusp of the first house.

Angle
The twelve houses of a chart are usually divided into three groups, called angles, **succedents**, and **cadents**. The angles comprise houses 1, 4, 7, and 10. A planet located in one of these houses is thought to act in a powerful and immediate way.

Aspect
An angular division between two planets or points is called aspect. Traditional astrology mainly uses the so-called Ptolemaic aspects, sextile, trine, square, and opposition. The conjunction, although technically not an aspect, is also often included for the sake of convenience.

Benefic
Part of a division, grouping planets into 'good' and 'bad' ones. Jupiter, Venus, Moon and Sun are seen to be benefic. It has to be noted though, that Mars and Saturn can achieve the status of benefics when in their **domicile**, **exaltation**, or **triplicity**. The other part of this division is called **malefic**.

Cadent
A house located furthest from an angular house in a anticlockwise motion is called cadent. Houses three, six, nine, and twelve are the cadent houses. A planet located in one of these houses is called a cadent planet and seen as weak. A planet can also be cadent from its own **domicile**, for example, Mars in Taurus.

Caput Algol
A malefic fixed star, often called the daemon star, positioned on the severed head Perseus is carrying. It is said to cause misfortune, violence and even death. Algol is known as 'the most evil star in the heavens'.

Caput Draconis
See **Dragon's Tail**

Cauda Draconis

See **Dragon's Head**

Cazimi

A planet is said to be cazimi when in a conjunction to the Sun, with an orb less than 16 or 17 minutes. This is also called 'in the heart of the Sun'. The planet is said to be strengthened by this conjunction.

Combust

A planet is said to be combust when it is between 17 minutes and 8.5 degrees away from the Sun. This is a debility and weakens the planet's influence.

Common Sign

Gemini, Pisces, Sagittarius, and Virgo are common, bi-corporeal signs, also known as mutable signs.

Cor Leonis

A beneficial fixed star, also known as Regulus, situated in the body of the Lion currently located at 0 degrees Virgo. This fixed star is one of the four Royal Stars of antiquity.

Cusp

The exact point where a house begins is called a cusp. It is the most powerful place of each house.

Debility

If a planet is placed in a sign where it is considered to be weak or afflicted it is debilitated (or in its debility). There are two essential **debilities**, called **detriment** and **fall**.

Detriment

The sign opposing a planet's **domicile** is the place of its detriment. It is one of the planets' essential **debilities** making the planet weak.

Dignity

If a planet is placed in a sign where it is considered to be strong, it is dignified (or in its dignity). There are five essential dignities: **domicile, exaltation, triplicity, term** and **face** (decanate).

Diurnal

A chart is diurnal if the Sun is located above the horizon, i.e. above the Ascendant-Descendant axis. Saturn, Jupiter, and the Sun are diurnal planets. Mercury is considered diurnal when **oriental**. These planets are more powerful during the day. Aries, Gemini, Leo, Libra, Sagittarius and Aquarius are diurnal signs.

Domicile

The sign over which a planet has rulership is called its domicile. Domicile rulership is the strongest essential **dignity**.

Dragon's Head

The Dragon's Head, also **Caput Draconis**, or **north lunar node**, is the point on the ecliptic where the Moon passes into northern latitude. Having the nature of Jupiter and Venus it is considered to be fortunate.

Dragon's Tail

The Dragon's Tail, also **Cauda Draconis**, or **south lunar node**, is the point on the ecliptic where the Moon passes into southern latitude. Thought to be of opposite nature to the Dragon's Head it is considered to be unfortunate.

Election

A chart drawn up for the most auspicious moment to undertake an event, usually chosen by the astrologer, is called an election.

Exaltation

A planet located in a sign wherein it is considered to be strong is called exalted. Exaltation is one of the five essential **dignities**.

Face

Face, also called decanate, is the name of one of the planets' weaker essential **dignities**. Beginning with Aries, the zodiac is divided into 36 faces, comprising 10 degrees each.

Fall

If a planet is located in the sign opposite that of its exaltation, it is said to be in its fall. This is one of the essential **debilities** rendering the planet weak.

Firdaria
A traditional astrological technique wherein individual planets rule certain periods of life.

Fixed Sign
Taurus, Leo, Scorpio and Aquarius are called fixed signs.

Geniture
Another name for a birth chart.

House Ruler
The planet that has **rulership** over the sign on a house **cusp** is called house ruler. The planet is also often said to be lord or lady of the house.

Luminaries
The Sun and the Moon are called luminaries.

Lunar North Node
See **Dragon's Head**

Lunar South Node
See **Dragon's Tail**

Medium Coeli
Also called midheaven, it is the zodiacal degree on which the celestial meridian falls. In most house systems this corresponds with the tenth house **cusp**.

Malefic
Saturn and Mars are seen to be malefic particularly when in their **detriment** or **fall**, or if they are **peregrine**. Any planet can be malefic when it has **rulership** over an unfortunate house.

Mutual Reception
Astrologers speak about mutual **reception** when a planet is in the **dignity** of another planet, and the latter one is also in the **dignity** of the former. For example, if Mars were in Taurus and Venus in Aries they would be in mutual **reception** by sign **rulership**.

Nocturnal
A chart is nocturnal if the Sun is below the horizon. Mars, Venus, and the Moon are nocturnal planets. This means that they are more powerful during the night. Taurus, Cancer, Virgo, Scorpio, Capricorn and Pisces are nocturnal signs.

Occidental
A planet is said to be occidental when it is rising after the Sun in the morning.

Oriental
A planet is said to be oriental when it is rising before the Sun in the morning.

Partile
An aspect between two planets is said to be partile if it is exact to the degree. For example, the Sun in 6 degrees Aries makes a partile opposition to Jupiter in 6 degrees Libra.

Peregrine
A planet with no essential **dignity** it is said to be peregrine.

Reception
When a planet is positioned in the place of the **dignity** of another, it is said to be received by the former. Reception can take place in any of the five dignities.

Retrograde
When a planet appears to be moving backwards, or anticlockwise, through the zodiac, such motion is called retrograde. The symbol for this is Rx.

Significator
A planet associated with the matter concerned is called significator.

Sign Ruler
Another name for a planet ruling over a sign of the zodiac, for example, Venus is Libra's diurnal ruler.

Spica
A beneficial fixed star situated in the Wheat Ear of Virgo currently located at 23 Libra.

Succedent

A house located next to an angular house in anticlockwise direction is called succedent. Houses 2, 5, 8, and 11 are succedent houses.

Syzygy

A term from the Greek referring to the New Moon or Full Moon. preceding one's birth, amongst other things.

Term

A sub-section of a sign which is one of the five essential **dignities**.

Triplicity

A group of three signs with the same nature is called a triplicity. Aries, Leo and Sagittarius comprise the fire triplicity and so forth.

Under the Sunbeams

A planet is said to be under the Sunbeams when it is between 8.5 degrees and 17 degrees away from the Sun. This has a debilitating effect, but less severe than the effect of **combustion**.

Via Combusta

An area located approximately between 15 degrees Libra and 15 degrees Scorpio which is believed to be an area of misfortune. There is some dispute amongst astrologers regarding the exact boundaries of the Via Combusta.

Zodiac

The virtual division of the ecliptic into twelve equal parts of 30 degrees forming the signs. Aries is considered to be the first sign of the zodiac.

Select Bibliography

Al-Biruni, *The Book of Instruction in the Elements of the Art of Astrology* (trans. R. Ramsey Wright), London: Luzac & Co, 1934.

Bingen, Hildegard von, *Physica* (trans. Priscilla Throop), Rochester: Healing Arts Press, 1989.

Cornford, Francis MacDonald, *Plato's Cosmology*, London: Routledge & Kegan Paul, 1948.

Culpeper, Nicholas, *Astrological Judgment of Diseases from the Decumbiture of the Sick*, London: Nathaniel Brookes, 1655.

Dee, John, *The Hieroglyphic Monad*, (trans. C. H. Josten), AMBIX, XII (1964), 84-221.

Ficino, Marsilio (trans. Kaske and Clark), *Three Books on Life*, Arizona: MRTS, 2002.

Greenbaum, Dorian Gieseler, *Temperament, Astrology's Forgotten Key*, Bornemouth: The Wessex Astrologer, 2005.

Hibner, Israel, *Mysterium Sigillorum, Herbarum & Lapidum*, London: W. Downing, 1698.

Iamblichus, *The Theology of Arithmetic* (trans. Robin Waterfield), Michigan: Phanes Press, 1988.

Kunz, George Frederick, *The Curious Lore of Precious Stones*, Philadelphia: J. P. Lippincott, 1913.

Lehman, Lee, *The Book of Rulerships*, Pennsylvania: Whitford Press, 1992.

Leonardi, Camilli, *Speculum Lapidum*, Venetia: 1502.

Lilly, William, *Christian Astrology*, London: Regulus Publishing, 1985.

Lorenz, Marie, *Die Okkulte Bedeutung der Edelsteine*, Leipzig: Verlag von Max Altmann, 1922.

Maplet, John, *A greene Forest, or a natural Historie*, London, Henry Denham, 1567.

Nettesheim, Heinrich Cornelius Agrippa von, *Magische Werke*, Vollständig in fünf Teilen, Wien: Amonesta Verlag, n.d.

Rensberger, Ferdinand: *Astronomia Teutsch*, Augsburg: Matthaeus Franck, 1569.

Robson, Vivian, *The Fixed Stars & Constellations in Astrology*, Abingdon: Astrology Classics, 2005.

Sättler-Musallam, Dr., *Das Geheimnis der 12 Edelsteine*, Berlin-Weissensee, Adonistischer Verlag, n.d.

Saunders, Richard, *The Astrological Judgment and Practice of Physick*, London: Langley Curtis, 1677.

Shumaker, Wayne, *John Dee on Astronomy*, California: University of California Press, 1978.

Wallis-Budge, Ernest Arthur, *Amulets and Talismans*, New York: University Books, 1968.

Westropp, Hodder Michael, *A Manual of Precious Stones and Antique Gems*, London: Sampson Low, Marston, Low, & Searle, 1874.

Index

CPSIA information can be obtained
at www.ICGtesting.com
Printed in the USA
BVHW01s2237150518
515768BV00017B/38/P